THE SCHOOL MA[...]

When the SMP was founded in [...]
radically new secondary-schoo[...]
sponding GCE and CSE syllabuses) to reflect, more adequately than
did the traditional syllabuses, the up-to-date nature and usages of
mathematics.

This objective has now been realized. SMP *Books 1–5* form a five-
year course to the O-level examination 'SMP Mathematics'. *Books
3T*, *4* and *5* give a three-year course to the same O-level examination
(the earlier *Books T* and *T4* being now regarded as obsolete). *Advanced
Mathematics Books 1–4* cover the syllabus for the A-level examination
'SMP Mathematics' and five shorter texts cover the material of the
various sections of the A-level examination 'SMP Further Mathematics'. There are two books for 'SMP Additional Mathematics' at
O-level. All the SMP GCE examinations are available to schools
through any of the Examining Boards.

Books A–H, originally designed as a CSE course, cover broadly
the same development of mathematics as do the first few books
of the O-level series. Most CSE Boards offer appropriate examinations. In practice, this series is being used very widely in
comprehensive schools, and its first seven books, followed by
Books X, *Y* and *Z* provide a course leading to the SMP O-level
examination.

Teacher's Guides accompany all these series of books.

The SMP has produced many other texts, and teachers are en-
couraged to obtain each year from the Cambridge University Press,
Bentley House, 200 Euston Road, London, NW1 2DB, the full list of
SMP books currently available. In the same way, help and advice
may always be sought by teachers from the Director at the SMP
Office, Westfield College, Hampstead, London, NW3 7ST, from which
may also be obtained the annual Reports, details of forthcoming
in-service training courses and so on.

The completion of this first ten years of work forms a firm base on
which the SMP will continue to develop its research into the mathematical curriculum. The team of SMP writers, numbering some forty
school and university mathematicians, is continually evaluating old
work and preparing for new. At the same time, the effectiveness
of the SMP's future work will depend, as it always has done, on
obtaining reactions from a wide variety of teachers – and also from
pupils – actively concerned in the class-room. Readers of the texts
can therefore send their comments to the SMP, in the knowledge
that they will be warmly welcomed.

ACKNOWLEDGEMENTS

The principal authors, on whose contributions the SMP texts are largely based, are named in the annual Reports. Many other authors have also provided original material, and still more have been directly involved in the revision of draft versions of chapters and books. The Project gratefully acknowledges the contributions which they and their schools have made.

This book – *Book X* – has been written by

T. Easterbrook   D. A. Hobbs
D. Hale   D. W. E. Lee
E. W. Harper   Thelma Wilson
Joyce Harris
and edited by Mary Tait.

The Project owes a great deal to its Secretaries, Miss Jacqueline Sinfield and Miss Julie Baker, for their careful typing and assistance in connection with this book.

We would especially thank Professor J. V. Armitage and P. G. Bowie for the advice they have given on the fundamental mathematics of the course.

Some of the drawings at the chapter openings in this book are by Ken Vail.

We are very grateful to the following for giving us permission to reproduce their material: ICL for punched cards and photographs of the paper tape reader (photograph by Geoffrey Sturdy Photography) and the visual display unit (photograph by Studio Jaanus Limited); Lloyds Bank Limited for a photograph of one of their cheques; the United States Information Service for the photograph of Mission Control, Houston; the Oxford and Cambridge Schools Examination Board and the Southern Regional Examinations Board for questions from their examination papers.

We are very much indebted to the Cambridge University Press for their cooperation and help at all times.

THE
SCHOOL
MATHEMATICS
PROJECT

Book X

CAMBRIDGE
AT THE UNIVERSITY PRESS

1972

Preface

This is the first of three books designed for O-level candidates who have previously followed the *A–H* series of books. *X*, *Y* and *Z* follow on from *Book G* and cover the remainder of the course for the O-level examination in 'SMP Mathematics'. The books will also be found suitable for students following a one year revision course for O-level and for those who have previously taken the CSE examination.

Many of the topics introduced in *Books A–G* are extended and dealt with in greater depth and several new topics are also introduced. *Book Z* contains review chapters covering the complete O-level course.

Many chapters in *Book X* discuss algebraic topics both from the manipulative and structural point of view. Set notation is introduced in Chapter 2 and used extensively in later chapters. The chapter on Functions introduces function notation, combinations of functions and inverses. In the Equations and Inequalities chapter the flow diagram method of solving equations has been temporarily abandoned in favour of a more 'direct' method to give students the opportunity to choose the method most suited to their needs and ability. This chapter is followed by the one on Formulas which stresses algebraic manipulation. The two chapters on Transformations revise earlier work from the *A–H* series and introduce combinations of transformations from a geometrical viewpoint. This work is complemented by the algebraic approach to the same topic in the chapter on Matrices and Transformations. Other chapters deal with 3D space, Computation (including standard index form), Vectors and the Areas of Irregular Figures. The Statistics chapter completes the work in Statistics required for the O-level course.

The chapters are interspaced with interludes and projects which are an integral part of the course but allow the student more freedom to experiment with mathematical ideas.

The three books will be accompanied by one Teacher's Guide to be published shortly after the publication of *Book Z*. The Teacher's Guide will contain answers, teaching suggestions and ideas. Until this book is published the SMP office will send duplicated sets of answers to teachers using the books. The address of the office can be found on p. i.

Contents

Contents

1 Thinking in three dimensions

This chapter is about three-dimensional geometry. It is not easy to visualize objects in three dimensions and it will help if you have the following apparatus:

a cardboard box;
a skeleton model of a box made with straws and pipecleaners;
a skeleton cube;
a skeleton square-based pyramid.

1 The adventures of Fred the fly in three dimensions

Investigation 1

Figure 1 shows a room. Fred, the mathematical fly, is in the top corner at F. Spike the spider is in a bottom corner at S.

Spike decides to stalk Fred by making his way along the edges of the room.

Thinking in three dimensions

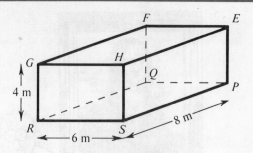

Fig. 1

(a) What is the shortest distance from S to F along the edges? How many such shortest routes are available?

(b) There are other longer routes. Find the length of the next longest route. How many routes are there of this length?

(c) Investigate the lengths of all the other possible routes, and find how many there are of each. (*Note*: Spike never goes through the same corner twice in any one attack on Fred.)

Investigation 2

Spike versus Fred again, but with different rules.

This time Spike walks diagonally across the carpet and then up the wall. See Figure 2(a).

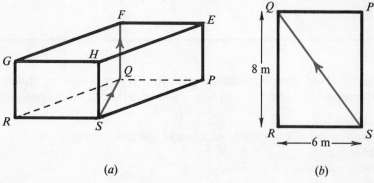

(a)   (b)

Fig. 2

To find how far he goes, look at Figure 2(b) which shows a fly's eye view of the floor. Use Pythagoras' rule to find the diagonal distance.

(a) How far does Spike go during this attack?

(b) There are two other routes of different lengths involving a diagonal and one edge. Find their lengths.

Investigation 3

Fred sometimes gets his revenge. When Spike is asleep Fred buzzes him. How far does Fred have to fly in order to reach Spike? It will help if you cut a triangle of paper as shown in Figure 3.

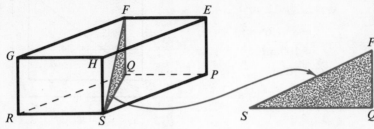

Fig. 3

The length of the base of this triangle is just the length of a diagonal of the floor – and you calculated this in Investigation 2. The height of the triangle is 4 m, the height of the room. Use Pythagoras' rule to find the distance which Fred has to fly.

Investigation 4

Spike decides to take the shortest route to Fred's corner, over the walls and over the floor or the ceiling, as necessary.

The problem is to find the length of this shortest route.
Try to work it out before you read on.
It will help to find the shortest route if you open out your box as in Figure 4.
The three points marked *F* fold up to make Fred's corner.
The shortest distance for Spike will be in a straight line. You will have to decide which of the three distances shown in Figure 4 is the shortest. You should be able to do it by using Pythagoras' rule.

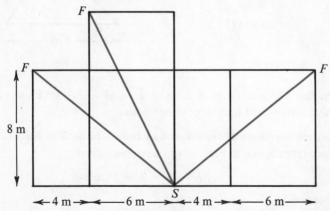

Fig. 4

Thinking in three dimensions

Pythagoras' rule in three dimensions

Look back at Investigation 3. Your solution might have been like this: from Figure 5,

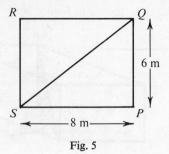

$$SQ^2 = SP^2 + PQ^2$$
$$= 8^2 + 6^2 \text{ m}^2$$
$$= 100 \text{ m}^2$$
$$SQ = 10 \text{ m}.$$

Fig. 5

From Figure 6,

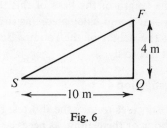

$$SF^2 = SQ^2 + QF^2$$
$$= 10^2 + 4^2 \text{ m}^2$$
$$= 116 \text{ m}^2$$
$$SF = 10 \cdot 8 \text{ m (3 s.f.).}$$

Fig. 6

The solution could have been written down more rapidly like this:

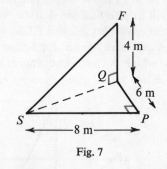

$$SF^2 = SQ^2 + QF^2$$
$$= (SP^2 + PQ^2) + QF^2$$
$$= 8^2 + 6^2 + 4^2 \text{ m}^2$$
$$= 116 \text{ m}^2$$
$$SF = 10 \cdot 8 \text{ m (3 s.f.).}$$

Fig. 7

You will see that SF^2 is the sum of three squares, $8^2 + 6^2 + 4^2$ (Figure 7). This is Pythagoras' rule extended into three dimensions.

(a) If the measurements of the room had been 5 m by 7 m by 3 m then the direct distance from Spike to Fred would have been given by:

$$SF^2 = 5^2 + 7^2 + 3^2 \text{ m}^2.$$

Find the distance SF.

(b) If a box measures 6 cm by 8 cm by 5 cm what is the direct distance between opposite corners?

Exercise A

1 A box measures 8 cm by 12 cm by 5 cm. See Figure 8.

(a) Calculate the lengths of
   (i) *AC*; (ii) *BG*; (iii) *BE*.

(b) Calculate the diagonal
   distance *BH*.

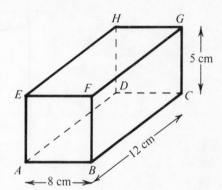

Fig. 8   ←—8 cm—→

2 Measure the edges of your box or straw model and calculate the direct distance from Spike's corner to Fred's corner. Check by measurement.

3 Measure the length, width and height of your classroom or a room at home. Calculate the Spike–Fred direct distance.

4 A garage is 5 m long, 3 m wide, 3 m high. Can a 7 m pole be stored in it? Explain your working.

5 If, in Investigation 4, Spike had been at the middle of the 6 m edge on the floor (the edge 'nearest' to you in Figures 1, 2, 3), calculate

(a) the direct distance from Spike to Fred through the air;
(b) the shortest distance over the walls and the floor or ceiling.

6 Fred is at one corner of a wedge and Spike at another. See Figure 9.

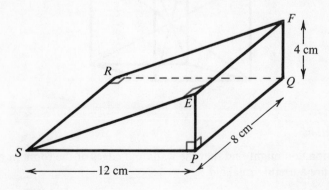

Fig. 9   ←————12 cm————→

(a) Calculate all the possible distances from S to F along the edges not passing through the same corner more than once.

(b) Calculate the direct distance across the sloping face.

7 Fred is at the top edge of a tin of baked beans. Spike is vertically below him at the bottom edge. See Figure 10. Spike craftily takes a diagonal route in

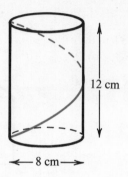

12 cm

←— 8 cm —→

Fig. 10

order to catch Fred by surprise. How far does Spike walk? (*Hint*: imagine the label opened out to make a rectangle. Using your slide rule calculate first the length of the rectangle.)

8 (a) A cube measures 5 cm by 5 cm by 5 cm. Find the length of a diagonal from one corner to the opposite one.

(b) Figure 11 shows how a cube can be split into six square-based pyramids. (You might have made a model of this earlier in the course.) Use your answer to (a) to find the length of one of the sloping edges of the pyramid.

   Make a sketch of the net for one of the pyramids and mark on it the dimensions.

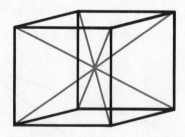

Fig. 11

2 Intersections

In this section you might find that the walls and edges of the room in which you are sitting are a useful visual aid.

(a) On a flat surface (that is, in two dimensions) two lines either intersect or are parallel. See Figure 12. For two lines in three dimensions what possibilities are there of intersection and non-intersection?

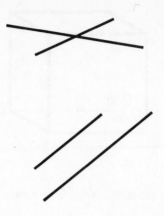

Fig. 12

Make a sketch of the room you are in and mark on it:

    (i) two lines which meet;
    (ii) two lines which are parallel;
    (iii) two lines which do not meet and are not parallel.

Such lines are called *skew* (as in skew-whiff).

(b) Using the room in which you are sitting give examples of:

    (i) two planes which meet;
    (ii) two planes which are parallel.

Is it possible to have two planes which do not meet and are not parallel? When two planes meet what is their intersection?

(c) Investigate the nature of the intersections of three planes. For example, can three planes intersect in a point, or in a line, or in two lines? Again, the room might help, but you might need to visualize some diagonal planes.

(d) There is just one straight line passing through two given points. How many planes are there passing through two given points?

How many planes are there passing through three given points?
How many planes contain a given line and a given point not on the line?
Is there always a plane passing through two given lines in three dimensions?

Thinking in three dimensions

A straw model of a cube will be helpful in this exercise. Imagine it labelled as in Figure 13.

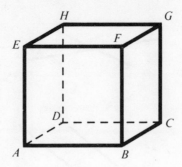

Fig. 13

1 Using Figure 13 name examples of the following:

   (a) two intersecting lines;
   (b) two parallel lines;
   (c) two skew lines which are at right angles;
   (d) two skew lines which are not at right angles;
   (e) two planes which intersect;
   (f) two planes which do not intersect;
   (g) three planes which intersect at a point;
   (h) three planes which intersect in two parallel lines.

2 Which of these pairs of lines determine a plane?

   (a) AB and CD;   (b) AB and HG;
   (c) AB and GC;   (d) EB and HC;
   (e) GF and DC;   (f) GB and ED.

3 Which of these sets of four points determine a plane?

   (a) A, B, C, D;   (b) A, B, G, H;
   (c) A, B, G, C;   (d) D, E, F, G;
   (e) B, D, F, H;   (f) C, D, F, H.

4 You might find a cube of plasticine useful in this question. If one of the corners of the cube in Figure 13 is cut off, a triangular section is obtained. See Figure 14. Show how to slice a cube in order to obtain a rectangular section. Repeat for the following sections:

   (a) trapezium;
   (b) hexagon;
   (c) pentagon.

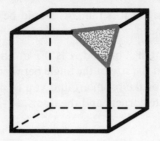

Fig. 14

3 Angles in three dimensions

(a) Angles between lines and planes

Each of the drawings in Figure 15 shows a thin pole stuck into the ground.

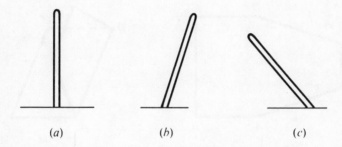

Fig. 15   (*a*)   (*b*)   (*c*)

Basil Brayne said: Figure 15(*a*) shows an upright pole. Figure 15(*b*) shows a pole making an angle of about 72° with the ground. Figure 15(*c*) shows a pole making an angle of about 50° with the ground. Was he right?

Think about it before you read on.

Basil Brayne was wrong! The drawings show the same pole. The angle depends on where you look from. Try it using a pen with one end on your paper.

Sometimes it is necessary to state the angle between a line and a plane, and in order to get agreement on which angle is measured it is done in this way:

Imagine a plumb-line attached to the top of the pole AB in Figure 16. Then, if it just touches the ground at C, the angle ABC is *the* angle between the pole and the ground.

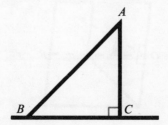

Fig. 16

Another way of thinking of it is that *BC* would be the shadow of the pole if the sun was directly overhead.

(*a*) If the pole is of length 2 m, and *A* is 0·7 m above the ground, use your trigonometry tables to find the size of the angle between the pole and the ground.

(*b*) Use a straw model or the room around you to pick out *the* angle between a diagonal joining opposite corners and the floor.

(b) Angles between planes

(*a*) Take a sheet of *unlined* paper and cut off two corners as shown in Figure 17(*a*). Then fold it as in Figure 17(*b*) to give two intersecting planes. Which is the angle between the two planes? Is it angle *BAF* or angle *CDE* or some other angle? Are these angles all equal?

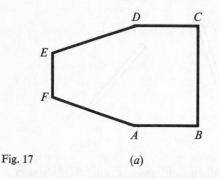 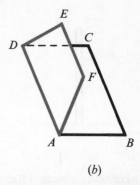

Fig. 17   (*a*)   (*b*)

(*b*) Repeat with a sheet of *lined* paper, making the fold at right-angles to the lines. Fold the paper flat and then open it to the position in Figure 17(*b*). The angle between the two parts of one of the lines on the paper is called *the angle between the planes*. Thus in Figure 17(*b*) neither of the angles *BAF* or *CDE* is the angle between the planes.

In order to find *the* angle between two planes it is necessary to have a line in each plane at right-angles to the line of intersection of the planes (the dotted lines in Figure 18). Then the angle between the planes is *PQR*.

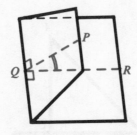

Fig. 18

(c) You will need a straw model of a square-based pyramid. See Figure 19 (the diagonals of the base have been marked in, O is vertically above N). Indicate which is the angle between the line OP and the plane PQRS. Show by attaching a piece of cotton to your model the angle between the planes OPQ and PQRS.

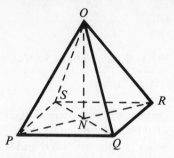

Fig. 19

Exercise C

Questions 1–6 refer to a cube labelled as in Figure 20. A straw model will be helpful.

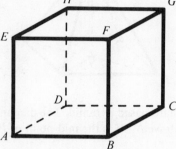

Fig. 20

1   Name the line of intersection of the planes:

    (a) ABCD and BCGF;   (b) ABCD and BCHE;
    (c) ABCD and BDHF;   (d) ADHE and EFGH.

2   State in each case in Question 1 the size of the angle between the planes.

3   Which of the following statements are true?

    (a) The angle between ADGF and EFGH is AFE;
    (b) the angle between ABGH and ABCD is GBD;
    (c) the size of the angle between CDEF and ABGH is 90°;
    (d) the size of the angle between ABCD and ACGE is 45°.

4   Name an angle which defines the angle between the following pairs of planes:

    (a) ABCD and ABGH;
    (b) ABGH and CDHG;
    (c) BDHF and ADHE;
    (d) ADGF and EFGH;
    (e) ADGF and BCGF.

5 Name in each case the angle between the line and the plane:

(a) *BG* and *ABCD*;
(b) *DF* and *ABCD*;
(c) *FG* and *ABGH*;
(d) *AG* and *CDHG*;
(e) *BH* and *ABFE*.

6 If the cube in Figure 20 has sides of length 5 cm calculate:

(a) the length of *AC*;
(b) the length of *AG*;
(c) the angle *AG* makes with the plane *ABCD*;
(d) the distance of *B* from the plane *ACGE*;
(e) the angle between the planes *AFGD* and *ABCD*.

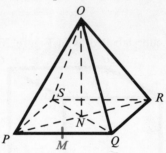

Fig. 21

Figure 21 shows a square-based pyramid. The diagonals of the base intersect at *N*. *O* is vertically above *N*. *M* is the mid-point of *PQ*.

You will find a straw model helpful in Questions 7 and 8.

7 (a) Name the line of intersection of the planes *OPR* and *OSQ*.
(b) What is the size of the angle between the planes *PQRS* and *OPR*?
(c) Name the angle between the planes *OPQ* and *PQRS*.

8 The sides of the square base are of length 5 cm. The sloping edges are of length 8 cm. Calculate the following:

(a) the length of *PR*;
(b) the length of *PN*;
(c) the height of *O* above *PQRS*;
(d) the angle between *OP* and the plane *PQRS*;
(e) the length of *OM*;
(f) the angle between the planes *OPQ* and *PQRS*.

4 Three-dimensional loci

(a) Spike and Mrs Spike are on the ceiling at *S* and *M*. See Figure 22.

S   M

Fig. 22

Fred decides to walk between them so that he is always equidistant from *S* and *M*. Describe his route.

(*b*) Suppose now he *flies* so that he is equidistant from *S* and *M*. Where are his possible positions?

The path of a moving point is often called a LOCUS (plural: LOCI). Thus in (*a*) Fred's locus is a straight line bisecting *SM* at right angles. In (*b*) the locus is a plane bisecting *SM* at right angles.

(*c*) Fred decides to 'buzz' Spike always keeping 10 cm away from him. What is his locus?

Exercise D

1 Two lines are drawn on a sheet of paper. See Figure 23. Draw a diagram showing the locus of a point which moves so that it is equidistant from the two lines.

Fig. 23

2 What is the locus of the point in Question 1 if it is not restricted to the plane of the paper?

3 *AB* is a line segment drawn on a sheet of paper. What is the locus of a point which moves in the plane of the paper so that its distance from the line segment is always 2 cm?

4 If *AB* is a line segment in space what is the locus of a point which moves so that its distance from *AB* is 2 cm?

5 Hold up a sheet of paper. What is the locus of a point which moves so that its distance from the paper is always 2 cm?

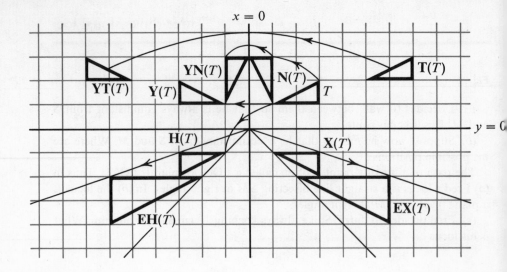

2 Combination of transformations I

1 Stencils and patterns

Fig. 1

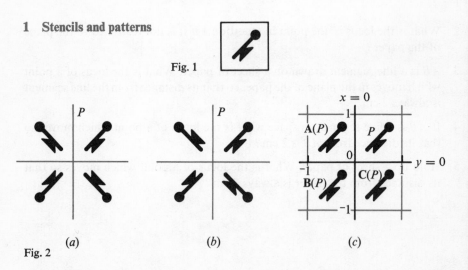

Fig. 2   (a)   (b)   (c)

(a) Figure 1 shows a stencil cut from a piece of card. It has been used to produce the patterns shown in Figure 2. Make a stencil of your own and use it to produce these patterns by the simple transformations of reflection, rotation and translation. You will need to perform three simple operations:

(i) tipping the stencil over about its edges (reflection);
(ii) turning the stencil in the plane of the paper with one corner fixed (rotation);
(iii) sliding the stencil along the paper (translation).

Keep your patterns for future use.

(*b*) The pattern in Figure 3 has been produced using a stencil of a triangle. Cut a stencil of a shape of your own choice and use it to produce some similar patterns. Think of what you are doing in terms of simple transformations, and try to discover some combined transformations which would give the same image as a single transformation. For example triangle *d* is the image of triangle *b* under a reflection in $x = 0$ followed by a reflection in $y = 0$, or simply by a half-turn about $(0,0)$.

Write down some of your findings.

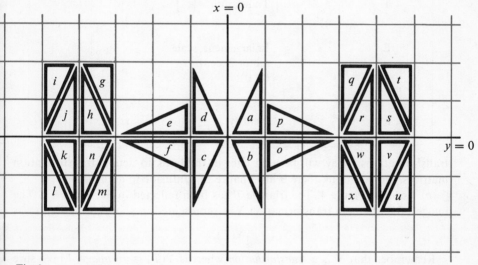

Fig. 3

2 A shorthand notation

See the table on the next page.

You might wonder why **X** denotes the transformation 'Reflection in $y = 0$' and **Y** denotes the transformation 'Reflection in $x = 0$'. This is because alternative names for the lines $y = 0$ and $x = 0$ are the x axis and the y axis respectively.

(*a*) Copy the table and leave space below it to add further information at a later stage. Leave the 'Inverse' column blank for the moment. You will need to refer back to the list during the course of this chapter and one further on in the book.

The capital letters in heavy type are used here as a shorthand method of writing

Combination of transformations I

Abbreviation	Transformation	Inverse
X	Reflection in $y = 0$ (i.e. in the x axis)	
Y	Reflection in $x = 0$ (i.e. in the y axis)	
Q	Anti-clockwise quarter- turn about (0, 0)	
H	Half-turn about (0, 0)	
T	Translation $\begin{pmatrix} 4 \\ 1 \end{pmatrix}$	
E	Enlargement, scale factor 2, centre (0, 0)	
I	Identity	

transformations. They will be used later in the book to denote transformation matrices. Do you think there is any chance of confusion in doing this?

(*b*) Look at Figure 4. The triangle T has been reflected in the line $x = 0$. The image of T after the transformation **Y** is represented in shorthand notation as

$$\mathbf{Y}(T).$$

Remember that **Y** is a *transformation* whereas **Y**(T) is an *image*. Make sure you understand this distinction before you continue.

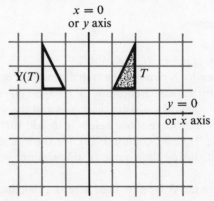

Fig. 4

(c) Copy Figure 4 and draw the images **X**(T) and **H**(T). Did you produce pattern (a) in Figure 2 in the same way? You might only have used reflections.

(d) On another copy of Figure 4 draw the images **I**(T), **T**(T), **Q**(T) and **E**(T). Try to use different colours for the images because some of them will overlap.

(e) **Y**(T) can be mapped back onto T by the transformation **Y**. Is there a listed transformation which maps

    (i) **X**(T) onto T;
    (ii) **H**(T) onto T;
    (iii) **Q**(T) onto T;
    (iv) **T**(T) onto T;
    (v) **E**(T) onto T;
    (vi) **I**(T) onto T?

(f) Add the following information to your list, and study Figure 5.

Abbreviation	Transformation	Inverse
U	Translation $\begin{pmatrix} {}^-4 \\ {}^-1 \end{pmatrix}$	
F	Enlargement, scale factor $\frac{1}{2}$, centre $(0, 0)$	
J	Clockwise quarter-turn about $(0, 0)$	

This information should enable you to complete (e) above.

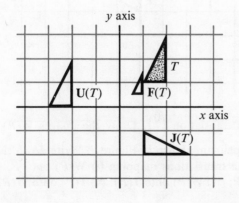

y axis

U(T) F(T) T

x axis

J(T)

Fig. 5

Combination of transformations I

1 On your copy of pattern (*b*) in Figure 2, label the images **Q**(*P*), **H**(*P*) and **J**(*P*).
   Which single transformations can be used to produce pattern (*b*) completely?

2 The images of pattern (*c*) have been labelled **A**(*P*), **B**(*P*) and **C**(*P*). Describe
   the transformations **A**, **B** and **C** accurately.

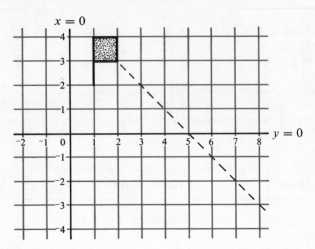

Fig. 6

3 **M** denotes a reflection in the line $x = 4$; **V** denotes an anti-clockwise quarter-
   turn about $(4, 1)$. Draw the images **M**(*F*) and **V**(*F*) where *F* is the flag shown
   in Figure 6. Describe the transformation which maps **M**(*F*) onto **V**(*F*) (the
   broken line will help you with your answer).
   Add **M** *and* **V** *to your list.*

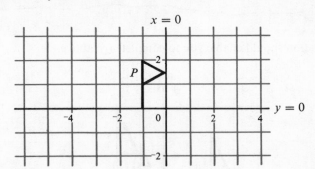

Fig. 7

4 **W** represents a translation $\binom{0}{1}$. Draw the images **W**(*P*), **T**(*P*) and **U**(*P*)
   where *P* is the pennant shown in Figure 7. Write down the column vectors
   which define the translations mapping (i) **W**(*P*) onto *P*; (ii) **T**(*P*) onto *P*;
   (iii) **U**(*P*) onto *P*; (iv) **W**(*P*) onto **T**(*P*); (v) **T**(*P*) onto **W**(*P*).

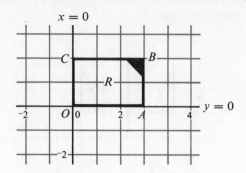

Fig. 8

5   **S** is a shear which leaves the points on the line $y = 0$ invariant and takes $(0, 1)$ to $(1, 1)$. **L** is a shear which leaves the points on the line $y = 0$ invariant and takes $(0, 1)$ to $(^-1, 1)$. Draw the images **S**(R) and **L**(R) where R is the rectangle in Figure 8. Which transformations will map (i) **S**(R) onto R; (ii) **L**(R) onto R? Can you give a meaning to **X**(**S**(R))? Draw the images **X**(**S**(R)) and **S**(**X**(R)).

   Add **S** *and* **L** *to your list.*

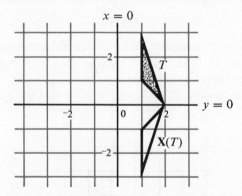

Fig. 9

6   Evaluate $\begin{pmatrix} 1 & 0 \\ 0 & ^-1 \end{pmatrix} \begin{pmatrix} 1 & 2 & 3 \\ 1 & 0 & 1 \end{pmatrix}$. Figure 9 shows a triangle T and its image **X**(T).

   What are the coordinates of the vertices of T? What does the 2×3 matrix represent? What transformation does the 2×2 matrix represent? What does your resultant matrix represent?

Summary

1   Capital letters in bold type (**X**, **Y**, **H**, ...) are used to represent *transformations*.
2   **X**(T) is the image of the object T after the transformation **X**.
3   If **A** takes F onto **A**(F) there is always a transformation which maps **A**(F) back onto F.

Combination of transformations I

3 Extending the shorthand notation

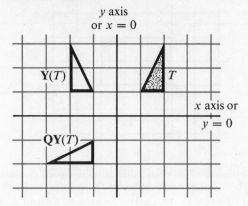

Fig. 10

(*a*) Look again at Figure 4 and then at Figure 10. Using our shorthand notation the image of triangle **Y**(*T*) after the transformation **Q** is

$$\mathbf{Q}(\mathbf{Y}(T)).$$

We usually omit the red brackets and write this more simply as

$$\mathbf{QY}(T).$$

QY(*T*) is therefore the image of *T* after *first* performing transformation **Y** and *then* transformation **Q**. You must remember that combined transformations must be read in 'Hebrew fashion' *from right to left*!

Draw a diagram to show *T*, **Q**(*T*) and **YQ**(*T*). Is **YQ**(*T*) the same image as **QY**(*T*)?

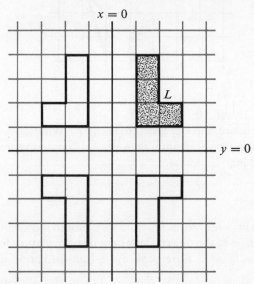

Fig. 11

20

(b) Copy Figure 11 and label the images **X**(*L*), **Y**(*L*), **XY**(*L*) and **YX**(*L*). You will notice that **XY**(*L*) and **YX**(*L*) are the same image. Now label **H**(*L*). We can write

$$\mathbf{XY}(L) = \mathbf{YX}(L) = \mathbf{H}(L).$$

What do the '=' signs mean here?

(c) **W** denotes the translation defined by $\begin{pmatrix} 2 \\ 0 \end{pmatrix}$.

Figure 12 shows a flag *F* and its image **XW**(*F*). This combined transformation is called a *glide-reflection*. Can you suggest why? Notice that the translation is parallel to the line of reflection.

We will use **G** to represent the combined transformation, so that

$$\mathbf{XW}(F) = \mathbf{G}(F).$$

Is **WX**(*F*) = **G**(*F*)? Can you find a *single* transformation which will map *F* onto **XW**(*F*)?

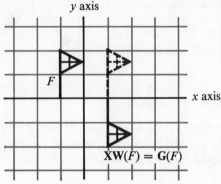

Fig. 12

(d) **A** denotes a one way stretch of 2 units parallel to *y* = 0. **B** denotes a one way stretch of 2 units parallel to *x* = 0.

Figure 13 shows **A**(*R*) and **B**(*R*), where *R* is the rectangle *PQST*. Copy Figure 13 and draw **AB**(*R*). Is **AB**(*R*) = **BA**(*R*)?

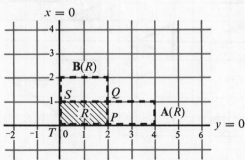

Fig. 13

Which single transformation from your list will map *R* onto **AB**(*R*)?

Combination of transformations I

1 P is the point $(3,1)$. Mark the images $\mathbf{X}(P)$; $\mathbf{Y}(P)$; $\mathbf{H}(P)$; $\mathbf{Q}(P)$; $\mathbf{E}(P)$; $\mathbf{T}(P)$; $\mathbf{XY}(P)$; $\mathbf{YE}(P)$; $\mathbf{EY}(P)$; $\mathbf{TX}(P)$; $\mathbf{XT}(P)$; $\mathbf{QX}(P)$; $\mathbf{XQ}(P)$. Write some 'equations' in which the '=' sign means 'is the same point as'.

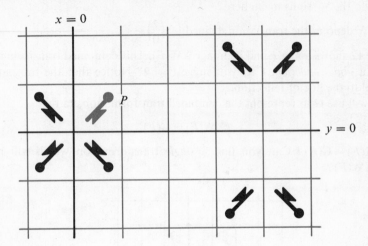

Fig. 14

2 Copy the pattern in Figure 14 (using your stencil if necessary) and label each image of P in shorthand notation.

3 Draw the images $\mathbf{U}(P)$, $\mathbf{T}(P)$, $\mathbf{UT}(P)$ and $\mathbf{TU}(P)$, where P is the pennant in Figure 7. Is $\mathbf{UT}(P) = \mathbf{TU}(P)$? Write down the column vectors defining the translations which map (i) P onto $\mathbf{UT}(P)$; (ii) P onto $\mathbf{TU}(P)$.

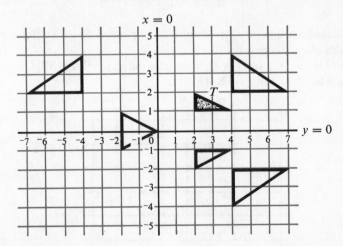

Fig. 15

4 Copy the diagram in Figure 15 and label the images $\mathbf{E}(T)$; $\mathbf{X}(T)$; $\mathbf{XE}(T)$; $\mathbf{XU}(T)$ and $\mathbf{EY}(T)$.

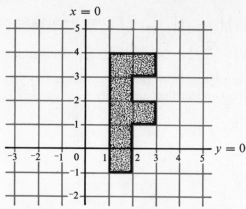

Fig. 16

5   Copy Figure 16 and draw the images **M**(*F*) and **YM**(*F*). If **N** denotes a reflection in *y* = 4 draw also the images **N**(*F*) and **XN**(*F*). Describe the single transformations which map (i) *F* onto **YM**(*F*); (ii) *F* onto **XN**(*F*). What do your answers suggest about successive reflections in two parallel lines?

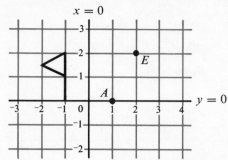

Fig. 17

6   In Figure 17 **B** denotes a quarter-turn about *A*. **D** denotes a clockwise quarter-turn about *E*. Draw the images **BD**(*F*) and **DB**(*F*), where *F* is the flag. Describe the single transformations which map (i) *F* onto **BD**(*F*); (ii) *F* onto **DB**(*F*).

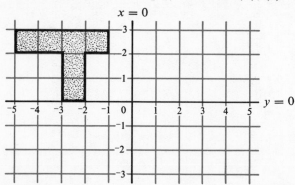

Fig. 18

7   Copy Figure 18. Draw the images **X**(*T*), **M**(*T*) and **YM**(*T*). Describe the single transformations which map (i) *T* onto **MX**(*T*); (ii) *T* onto **YM**(*T*).

8   Evaluate $\begin{pmatrix} 1 & 0 \\ 0 & ^{-}1 \end{pmatrix} \begin{pmatrix} ^{-}1 & 0 \\ 0 & 1 \end{pmatrix} \begin{pmatrix} 1 & 2 & 1 \\ 1 & 1 & 3 \end{pmatrix}$. Draw the triangle with vertices defined

by the matrix $\begin{pmatrix} 1 & 2 & 1 \\ 1 & 1 & 3 \end{pmatrix}$. Describe the transformations which the above

2×2 matrices represent. Draw the triangle defined by your resultant matrix. Explain what has happened geometrically.

3 Sets

1 The universal set

(*a*) If $A = \{$king of hearts, king of diamonds$\}$, which elements do not belong to the set A?

The answer depends on what objects we wish to consider. For example, if we are concerned with the kings in a standard pack of fifty-two playing cards then the list would contain two elements: the king of spades and the king of clubs.

How many elements would the list contain if we were considering (i) the picture cards in the pack, (ii) the red cards in the pack, (iii) the red kings in the pack, (iv) the objects in the drawing at the head of this chapter?

We call the set of all the elements which we wish to consider the *universal set* and denote it by $\mathscr{E}$. $\mathscr{E}$ is always written in curly script and is an abbreviation for *ensemble*, the French word for set. In a diagram we usually show the universal set as a rectangle.

Sets

(b) Those elements of $\mathscr{E}$ which are not elements of A form another set. We call this set the *complement* of A and denote it by A'. Copy Figure 1 and shade the region which represents A'.

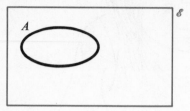

Fig. 1   Fig. 2

If $\mathscr{E} = \{$kings in the pack$\}$ then $A' = \{$king of spades, king of clubs$\}$. See Figure 2.

If $\mathscr{E} = \{$objects in the picture at the head of this chapter$\}$, list the members of A' and draw a diagram to illustrate your answer.

If $\mathscr{E} = \{$red kings in the pack$\}$, how many elements are there in A'?

We call the set which contains no elements the *empty set* and denote it by $\varnothing$. So, in the last example, $A' = \varnothing$.

$\varnothing$ is a Danish letter and is pronounced 'oe'.

Exercise A

1 Let $0 = \{$odd numbers$\}$.

    (a) List the members of 0 if $\mathscr{E} = \{4, 5, 6\}$.

    (b) List the members of 0 if $\mathscr{E} = \{$positive whole numbers less than 15$\}$.

    (c) List the members of 0 if $\mathscr{E} = \{$whole numbers n such that $25 < n < 40\}$.

2 If $\mathscr{E} = \{1, 2, 3, 4, 5, 6, 7\}$ and $X = \{2, 5, 6\}$, list the members of X' and draw a diagram like the one in Figure 2 to illustrate your answer.

3 If $\mathscr{E} = \{$positive even numbers less than 10$\}$ and $Y = \{$multiples of 4$\}$, list the members of (a) Y, (b) Y'.

4 Let $\mathscr{E} = \{^-3, ^-2, ^-1, 0, 1, 2, 3\}$.

    (a) List the members of A' if $A = \{^-2, 0, 2\}$.

    (b) If $B' = \{$positive numbers$\}$, list the members of B.

5 If $R = \{1, 5\}$ and $R' = \{2, 6, 8\}$, list the members of $\mathscr{E}$ and draw a diagram to illustrate your answer.

6 If $P = \{1, 7\}$ and $Q = \{3, 9, 17\}$, define a possible universal set.

7 If $\mathscr{E} = \{$letters of the English alphabet$\}$ and $A = \{$letters in the sentence 'The quick brown fox jumps over the lazy dog.'$\}$, what can you say about A'?

26

8   If $\mathscr{E} = \{1,2,3,4\}$ and $X = \{4\}$, list the members of (a) the complement of X, (b) the complement of the complement of X.

9   Write in a simpler form: (a) $\varnothing'$; (b) $(A')'$.

2   Notation

Let

$\mathscr{E} = \{$cards in a standard pack of 52 playing cards$\}$,

$P = \{$picture cards$\}$,

$Q = \{$queens$\}$,

$R = \{$red cards$\}$.

(a) Curly brackets are shorthand notation for 'the set of'.

We can define a set either by describing it in words or by listing all its members. For example:

$Q = \{$queens$\}$

or $Q = \{Q \clubsuit, Q \diamondsuit, Q \heartsuit, Q \spadesuit\}$.

(b) We write $n(Q) = 4$ as shorthand for 'the number of members or elements of Q is 4'.

Write down (i) $n(\mathscr{E})$, (ii) $n(R)$, (iii) $n(P')$, (iv) $n(\varnothing)$.

Define a set S such that $n(S) = 13$.

(c) The symbol $\in$ is shorthand for 'is a member of' or 'is an element of', so

$$2 \heartsuit \in R.$$

Suggest a meaning for

$$3 \spadesuit \notin R.$$

Is it true that

$$3 \spadesuit \in R' ?$$

If $S = \{$spades$\}$, is it true that

$$3 \spadesuit \in S?$$

(d) Figure 3 shows how P and Q are related.

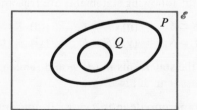

Fig. 3

Since *every* member of Q is also a member of P, we say that Q is a *subset* of P and write

$$Q \subset P.$$

Is Q a subset of $\mathscr{E}$?

Do you agree that $Q \subset Q$ and that $\varnothing \subset Q$?

Which of the following statements are true: (i) $R \subset \mathscr{E}$; (ii) $Q \subset R$; (iii) $S \subset R'$; (iv) $\varnothing \subset R$; (v) $P' \subset Q'$?

(*e*) We sometimes say that P contains Q and write

$$P \supset Q.$$

If $D = \{\text{diamonds}\}$, is it true that $R \supset D$? Draw a diagram to show how $\mathscr{E}$, D and R are related.

Relations such as $Q \subset P$ and $P \supset Q$ are called *inclusion relations*.

(*f*) Be careful not to confuse $\in$ with $\subset$. Remember that an element $\in$ or $\notin$ a set and a set $\subset$ or $\not\subset$ another set. For example:

$$K \spadesuit \in P$$

but

$$\{K \spadesuit\} \subset P.$$

Exercise B

1   Describe in words each of the following sets:

(*a*) $\{7 \clubsuit, 7 \diamondsuit, 7 \heartsuit, 7 \spadesuit\}$;

(*b*) $\{A \diamondsuit, A \heartsuit\}$;

(*c*) R', where $R = \{\text{red cards}\}$ and $\mathscr{E} = \{\text{cards in a standard pack of 52 playing cards}\}$;

(*d*) P', where $P = \{\text{picture cards}\}$ and $\mathscr{E} = \{\text{cards in a standard pack of 52 playing cards}\}$.

2   Let $\mathscr{E} = \{\text{counting numbers less than 20}\}$, $T = \{\text{multiples of three}\}$, $F = \{\text{multiples of 5}\}$ and $S = \{\text{multiples of 6}\}$.

(*a*) List the members of T, F and S.

(*b*) Write down (i) $n(\mathscr{E})$; (ii) $n(T)$; (iii) $n(F)$; (iv) $n(S)$.

(*c*) Copy Figure 4 and write each of the numbers from 1 to 19 in the appropriate region.

(*d*) Which of the following statements are true and which are false?

(i) $S \subset \mathscr{E}$;   (ii) $F \subset T$;   (iii) $S \subset T$;

(iv) $T \supset S$;   (v) $S \subset F'$;   (vi) $S' \supset F$.

(*e*) Which of the statements in (*d*) would remain true if $\mathscr{E} = \{\text{counting numbers less than 32}\}$?

Would Figure 4 be appropriate in this case? If not, draw a correct diagram.

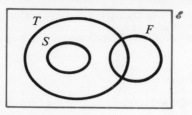

Fig. 4

3 Let $\mathscr{E}$ = {letters of the English alphabet} and V = {vowels}.

   (a) State (i) $n(\mathscr{E})$, (ii) $n(V')$.
   (b) Write down a subset of V'.
   (c) Define a set A such that $A \subset V$ and $n(A) = 2$.
   (d) Write down *all* the subsets of V which have 4 elements.

4 Copy each of the following pairs and insert the correct symbol $\in$, $\notin$, $\subset$ or $\not\subset$ between them.

   (a) {3}   {counting numbers};
   (b) 3   {counting numbers};
   (c) 3   {even numbers};
   (d) {3}   {even numbers};
   (e) {4, 6}   {even numbers};
   (f) 4, 5, 6   {counting numbers};
   (g) {4, 5, 6} {counting numbers}.

5 (a) List all the subsets of {Alan, Brenda, Charles}. Remember to count the empty set and the original set as subsets.
   (b) How many subsets has a set with (i) one member, (ii) two members, (iii) three members? Guess the number of subsets of a set with four members and then check whether your guess is correct.
   If a set has ten members, how many subsets would you expect it to have?

6 {Alan, Brenda} has 1 subset with no members, 2 subsets with one member and 1 subset with two members.
   Use your answer to Question 5(a) to help you to write down the number of subsets of {Alan, Brenda, Charles} which have (i) no members, (ii) one member, (iii) two members, (iv) three members.
   Now write down the number of subsets of {Alan, Brenda, Charles, David} which have (i) no members, (ii) one member, (iii) two members, (iv) three members, (v) four members.
   Where have you seen this number pattern before? Use it to guess the number of subsets of {Alan, Brenda, Charles, David, Edna} which have three elements.

7 (a) Define three sets A, B and C such that $A \subset B$ and $B \subset C$. Is A a subset of C?
   (b) If A, B and C are any three sets such that $A \subset B$ and $B \subset C$, is it always,

29

sometimes, or never true that (i) $A \subset C$, (ii) $A' \supset C'$, (iii) $C \subset A$?

8   Is it possible to find a, X and $\mathscr{E}$ such that $a \in X$ and $a \in X'$?

3   Union and intersection

Let $\mathscr{E}$ = {cards in a standard pack of 52 playing cards},

A = {aces}, B = {black cards},
C = {clubs}, D = {diamonds},
P = {picture cards}, Q = {queens},
X = {A ♣, 2 ♣, 3 ♣, 4 ♣, 5 ♣}, Y = {2 ♣, 3 ♣, 5 ♣, J ♣}.

(*a*) The shaded region in Figure 5 represents the *union* of the two sets A and D. This set, written $A \cup D$, is the set of members of *A or D or both.*

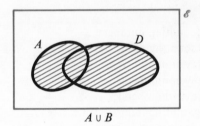

Fig. 5 $A \cup B$

Note that although the ace of diamonds is a member of both A and D, it is listed only once in $A \cup D$. So $n(A \cup D) = 16$.

List the members of $X \cup Y$. Do you agree that $n(X \cup Y) = 6$?

(*b*) List the elements which belong to both A and B. Describe this set in words.

The set of elements which belong to both A and B is the intersection of A and B and is denoted by $A \cap B$. So

$$A \cap B = \{\text{black aces}\}$$

or

$$A \cap B = \{\text{A ♣, A ♠}\}.$$

List the elements which belong to $A \cap B'$. How would you describe this set?

In Figure 6, the region ① represents $A \cap B$ and the region ② represents $A \cap B'$. What sets do the regions ③ and ④ represent?

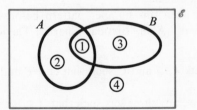

Fig. 6

Do you agree that region ④ represents $A' \cap B'$? Do you agree that it also represents $(A \cup B)'$?

List the members of (i) $X \cap Y$, (ii) $X' \cap Y$, (iii) $X \cap Y'$.

State (i) $n(X \cap Y)$, (ii) $n(X \cap Y')$, (iii) $n(X' \cap Y)$, (iv) $n(X' \cap Y')$, (v) $n(X \cup Y)$, (vi) $n(X \cup Y)'$. Your answers to (iv) and (vi) should be the same. Why?

(c) Draw a diagram to show how B, C and $\mathscr{E}$ are related.

Which set is equal to $B \cap C$? Which set is equal to $B \cup C$?

Because all clubs are black, you should have found that $B \cap C = C$ and $B \cup C = B$.

Notice that the statement 'all clubs are black' can be written in symbols as $C \subset B$.

(d) Figure 7 shows the relations between C, D and $\mathscr{E}$.

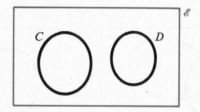

Fig. 7

State $n(C \cap D)$ and name the set which is equal to $C \cap D$.

Two sets, such as C and D, which have no members in common are called *disjoint*.

Notice that the statement 'no clubs are diamonds' can be written in symbols as $C \cap D = \varnothing$.

We have already seen that the sets A and B are not disjoint, so $A \cap B \neq \varnothing$. This is equivalent to the statement 'some aces are black'.

(e) Write the following statements in simple English: (i) $B \cap D = \varnothing$; (ii) $D \subset B'$; (iii) $P \cap C \neq \varnothing$.

(f) Write the following statements in symbols: (i) all queens are picture cards; (ii) some aces are red; (iii) no aces are queens.

Exercise C

1 If $A = \{a,b,c,d\}$ and $B = \{a,c,e\}$, list the members of (a) $A \cap B$; (b) $A \cup B$.

2 If $E = \{4,6,8,10,12,14,16\}$ and $F = \{2^2, 2^3, 2^4\}$, list the members of (a) $E \cap F$; (b) $E \cup F$.
   Write down an inclusion relation satisfied by E and F.

3 If $\mathscr{E} = \{1,2,3,4,5,6\}$, $P = \{5,2,1\}$ and $Q = \{5,4,3,2\}$, list the members of (a) P'; (b) Q'; (c) $P' \cap Q'$; (d) $(P \cup Q)'$.

4 If $\mathscr{E} = \{\text{natural numbers}\}$, $X = \{1,3,5,7,9,11\}$ and $Y = \{1,2,4,5,9,10\}$, write down (a) $X \cup Y$; (b) $X \cap Y'$; (c) $Y \cap X'$.

5   If $\mathscr{E} = \{a,b,c,d,e\}$, give suitable examples of sets A and B such that
    (a) $A \cap B = \varnothing$; (b) $A \subset B$.

6   Use set notation to describe the shaded region in each of the diagrams in
    Figure 8.

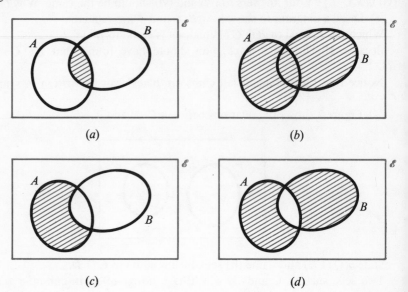

(a)   (b)

Fig. 8   (c)   (d)

7   Is it always, sometimes or never true that $(A \cap B) \subset (A \cup B)$?

8   What can you say about sets P and Q if (a) $P \cap Q = P$; (b) $P \cup Q = Q$?
    Are these two statements equivalent?

9   Simplify:

   (a) $A \cup A$; (b) $A \cap A$; (c) $A \cup \mathscr{E}$;
   (d) $A \cap \mathscr{E}$; (e) $A \cup \varnothing$; (f) $A \cap \varnothing$;
   (g) $\varnothing \cup \mathscr{E}$; (h) $\varnothing \cap \mathscr{E}$.

10 Is it always, sometimes or never true that:

   (a) $P \cup Q = Q \cup P$; (b) $P \cap Q = Q \cap P'$;
   (c) $P \cup Q = P \cap Q$; (d) $(P \cap Q)' = P' \cup Q'$?

11 Simplify:

   (a) $(A' \cap B')'$; (b) $A \cap B \cap A'$; (c) $(A \cap B) \cup (A \cap B')$.

12 If $\mathscr{E} = \{\text{all people}\}$, define three suitable sets F, G and H and draw a diagram
    to illustrate the statement 'no fourth form girl can ride a horse'.

13 If $\mathscr{E} = \{\text{animals}\}$, $C = \{\text{cats}\}$ and $W = \{\text{wild animals}\}$, write a sentence
    equivalent to the statement $C \cap W \neq \varnothing$.

14 If $n(M) = 11$, $n(N) = 7$ and $n(M \cap N) = 5$, state the value of $n(M \cup N)$.

15 If $\mathscr{E} = \{$birds$\}$, $P = \{$birds which cannot fly$\}$ and $Q = \{$female birds$\}$, describe in words each of the two sets $P' \cap Q$ and $P \cap Q'$.

16 If $\mathscr{E} = \{$natural numbers$\}$, $A = \{$odd numbers$\}$ and $B = \{$multiples of 5$\}$, describe the set $B \cap A'$.

17 Let $\mathscr{E} = \{$birds alive at this moment$\}$, $C = \{$canaries$\}$, $S = \{$singing birds$\}$ and $W = \{$well-fed birds$\}$.

  (*a*) Write a sentence equivalent to each of the following statements:
  (i) $C \subset S$; (ii) $S \subset C$; (iii) $S \cap W \cap C' = \varnothing$.
  (*b*) Write each of the following sentences in symbols:

     (i) Some canaries are well-fed.
     (ii) Some singing canaries are not well-fed.
     (iii) No ill-fed canaries sing.

4 Venn diagrams

(*a*) In a class of 33 pupils, 18 study Russian, 23 study German and 11 study both these languages. Try to work out how many pupils do not learn either language.

Diagrams like those in Figures 1 to 8 which show the relations between sets are called Venn diagrams after John Venn (1834–1923), a Cambridge mathematician.

Although you were probably able to solve the problem in (*a*) without the aid of a diagram, you will find that for more complicated problems about sets of objects a Venn diagram is often helpful.

(*b*) Let us look again at the problem in (*a*).

Before we can draw a diagram, we must define some suitable sets:

$$\mathscr{E} = \{\text{pupils in the class}\},$$
$$R = \{\text{pupils who study Russian}\},$$
$$G = \{\text{pupils who study German}\}.$$

Copy Figure 9 which shows the relations between $\mathscr{E}$, R and G, and the information given in the problem.

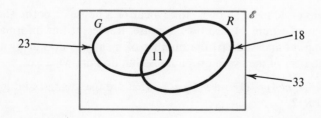

Fig. 9

Sets

You should now be able to see why $n(G \cap R') = 12$ and $n(R \cap G') = 7$. Enter these numbers in the appropriate regions of your diagram and use the fact that $n(\mathscr{E}) = 33$ to find $n(G' \cap R')$.

Do you agree that 3 pupils learn neither Russian nor German?

(b) Look carefully at Figure 10 and make sure that you understand why the whole of the shaded region represents $B \cap C$, the region ① represents $B \cap C \cap D$ and the region ② represents $B \cap C \cap D'$.

What sets do the other labelled regions represent?

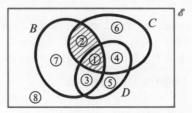

Fig. 10

(c) Of 50 people who were interviewed 32 said that they looked at BBC 1, 33 that they looked at ITV and 13 that they looked at BBC 2. Nine of the people asked said that they looked at BBC 1 *and* BBC 2 and, of these, 5 looked at ITV as well. Three looked only at BBC 2 and 12 only at ITV.

Copy Figure 10 leaving out the red shading and the labels ① to ⑧. If

$$\mathscr{E} = \{\text{people interviewed}\},$$
$$B = \{\text{people who looked at BBC 1}\},$$
$$C = \{\text{people who looked at BBC 2}\}$$

and

$$D = \{\text{people who looked at ITV}\},$$

enter the number of elements in each region of your diagram.

(You are advised to consider the regions in the order ①, ②, ⑥, ⑤, ④, ③, ⑦, ⑧.)

Do you agree that 2 people said that they never looked at television? If not, try again.

Use your Venn diagram to help you to write down (i) the number of people who said that they looked only at BBC 1, (ii) the number of people who said that they looked at BBC 1 and ITV but not at BBC 2.

Exercise D

1 In a group of 40 men, 38 own either a car or a house or both. There are 33 car owners of whom 24 also own a house. Represent this information on a Venn diagram and state (i) the number of men who do not own a house, (ii) the number of men who own a house but do not own a car.

2 If $n(\mathscr{E}) = 24$, $n(A) = 11$ and $n(B) = 7$, what are the greatest and least values of $n(A \cup B)$?

34

Draw Venn diagrams to illustrate the cases in which $n(A \cup B)$ has these extreme values.

3   In a party of girls it was noticed that:

(i) all girls wearing jeans were wearing boots;
(ii) no girl wearing jeans had long hair;
(iii) some girls wearing boots had long hair.

(a) Using J, B, L for the three sets involved, draw a Venn diagram.
(b) Put a cross in your diagram to represent a long-haired girl wearing sandals.
(c) Express the statements (i), (ii) and (iii) in symbols.

4   In an athletics test involving 70 pupils, standards were awarded as follows: sprinting 31; jumping 29; throwing 36; sprinting and throwing 12; all three events 5; jumping only 7; throwing only 15. Define suitable sets $\mathscr{E}$, S, J and T and represent the given information on a Venn diagram.

State (i) the number of pupils gaining sprinting standards only, (ii) the number of pupils gaining standards in exactly two events, (iii) the number of pupils who did not gain any standards.

5   In a group of 30 boys, 19 have played rugby, 17 have played soccer and 10 have played both; three of these ten have also played basket-ball. Five boys have played soccer and basket-ball and nine have played rugby and basket-ball. All the boys have played at least one of these games. Represent this information on a Venn diagram and state the number of boys who have played basket-ball only.

6   The police are investigating the passing of counterfeit money last Saturday evening at three coffee bars: The Peacock, The Quest and The Rajah. There are 11 suspects and the police have discovered the following facts:

(i) 5 of the suspects visited The Peacock;
(ii) 4 remained in The Rajah all the evening but 3 others looked in – these 3 visited all three of the coffee bars;
(iii) 6 visited The Quest;
(iv) 1 remained out of town all the evening.

(a) Using P, Q, R for the three sets involved, draw a Venn diagram to show all the known facts.
(b) State (i) $n(P \cup Q)$; (ii) $n(R')$; (iii) $n(Q \cap R \cap P')$.
(c) How many suspects visited The Peacock and The Quest but not The Rajah?
(d) Express the statements (iii) and (iv) in symbols.

7   One hundred and twenty people attended a mixed hockey club dance. Forty-seven were men over 25 years old of whom 15 still played hockey. There were 24 players under 25 of whom 9 were women. 75 of those present were

35

over 25 years of age and 41 of those present played hockey. There were 10 more men than women. If $\mathscr{E} = \{\text{people present}\}$, $T = \{\text{people over 25}\}$, $M = \{\text{men}\}$ and $H = \{\text{people who play hockey}\}$, represent the given information on a Venn diagram.

Could the women who were present raise a team of 11 players?

How many of the men who were present did not play hockey?

8 Teletown is a fringe area. $\mathscr{E} = \{\text{houses in Teletown}\}$, $A = \{\text{houses receiving BBC 1 clearly}\}$, $B = \{\text{houses receiving BBC 2 clearly}\}$ and $C = \{\text{houses receiving ITV clearly}\}$. Describe the sets $A \cap B$, $A' \cap B'$, $A \cup B$ and $A \cup B \cup C$.

If A, B, $C \subset \mathscr{E}$, $n(\mathscr{E}) = 1000$, $n(A) = 500$ and $n(B) = 400$, give the greatest and least values of $n(A \cup B)$ and $n(A \cap B)$.

If $n(A \cap C) = 200$, what (if anything) can you say about $n(C)$?

5 Loci

Since a locus is a set of points, we often use set notation to describe loci.

(a) Figure 11 shows $\{x : {}^-2 \leqslant x < 4\}$. This is read as 'the set of numbers x such that x is greater than or equal to $^-2$ and less than 4'.

Notice that the colon stands for 'such that'.

Fig. 11

Use set notation to describe the set of numbers x such that x is greater than $^-3$ and less than 1.

Write down three members of $\{x : 0 < x < \frac{1}{2}\}$.

Draw a diagram to illustrate $\{x : x > 1\}$.

(b) The shaded region in Figure 12 can be described as $A = \{(x, y) : x + y > 2\}$. This is read as '$A$ is the set of points (x, y) such that $x + y > 2$.'

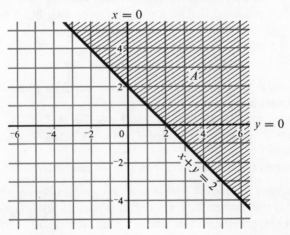

Fig. 12

36

Use set notation to describe (i) the unshaded region in Figure 12, (ii) the set of points on the line $x + y = 2$.

Sketch a diagram similar to that in Figure 12 to show $\{(x, y): x > 1\}$. Why is this diagram different from the one which you drew for $\{x: x > 1\}$ in (a)?

(c) In two dimensions the locus of a point F such that $SF = MF$, where S and M are fixed points, is the mediator of SM, that is a straight line bisecting SM at right angles. (See Figure 13.) We write this locus as $\{F: SF = MF\}$.

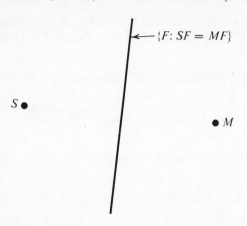

Fig. 13

Describe the locus $\{F: SF = MF\}$ in three dimensions. If you have difficulty, look back at Chapter 1, section $4(b)$.

In two dimensions the universal set is a plane; in three dimensions it is the whole of space.

Describe the locus $\{F: SF = 10 \text{ cm}\}$ in (i) two dimensions, (ii) three dimensions.

Describe the locus $\{F: SF \geqslant 10 \text{ cm}\}$ in (i) two dimensions, (ii) three dimensions.

Exercise E

1   Let $\mathscr{E} = \{x: {}^-3 \leqslant x \leqslant 3\}$, $P = \{x: x \geqslant {}^-1\}$ and $Q = \{x: x < 2\}$.

    (a) Draw separate diagrams similar to the one in Figure 11 to illustrate (i) P, (ii) Q, (iii) $P \cap Q$.

    (b) Write down an expression for $P \cap Q$.

2   By sketching diagrams similar to the one in Figure 12, show:

    (a) $\{(x, y): y > 2x\}$; (b) $\{(x, y): {}^-2 < x < 1\}$;

    (c) $\{(x, y): 0 > y > {}^-2\}$; (d) $\{(x, y): x + 2y < 4\}$.

3   Mark on a diagram the boundaries of the regions $A = \{(x, y): 1 \leqslant x \leqslant 4\}$ and $B = \{(x, y): 0 \leqslant y \leqslant x\}$ and shade the region $A \cap B$.

4   Draw a diagram to show by shading the set $P \cap Q$, where $P = \{(x, y): x > 3\}$ and $Q = \{(x, y): x > y\}$.

5 If $S = \{(x, y): 2y - x = 6\}$, verify that $(0, 3) \in S$ and write down four other members of S.

6 Let $\mathscr{E} = \{x: {}^-4 \leqslant x \leqslant 3\}$, $A = \{x: {}^-4 < x < 3\}$, $B = \{x: {}^-2 < x \leqslant 1\}$ and $C = \{x: 1 \leqslant x < 2\}$.

    (a) Draw separate diagrams to illustrate (i) $\mathscr{E}$, (ii) A, (iii) B, (iv) C.
    (b) Write down expressions for (i) A', (ii) $B \cap C$, (iii) $B \cup C$, (iv) $B \cap A'$.

7 If $\mathscr{E} = \{x: {}^-2 \leqslant x \leqslant 6\}$, $L = \{x: 1 \leqslant x \leqslant 6\}$, $M = \{x: {}^-2 \leqslant x < 2\}$ and $N = \{x: 0 < x \leqslant 3\}$, write similar expressions for (a) $L \cap M$, (b) M', (c) $L \cap N$, (d) $L \cap N \cap M'$.

8 A and B are the points $(2, 0)$ and $(6, 0)$ respectively. State the coordinates of four members of $\{P: AP = BP\}$.

9 Mark a point A and sketch the locus $\{P: AP < 2 \text{ cm}\}$ in the plane of your paper.

10 Mark a point B and sketch the locus $\{P: 3 \text{ cm} < BP < 5 \text{ cm}\}$ in the plane of your paper.

11 If A is the point $({}^-2, 0)$ and B is the point $(2, 0)$, sketch or describe the locus $\{P: AP \geqslant BP\}$.

12 Draw a straight line segment of length 3 cm. Sketch the locus in the plane of your paper of $\{P: \text{the distance from } P \text{ to the nearest point on } AB \text{ is 2 cm}\}$.

13 P is the set of points inside the rectangle shown in Figure 14.
    Sketch the rectangle and the boundaries of X and Y where $X = \{P: AP > 3 \text{ cm}\}$ and $Y = \{P: CP > DP\}$.
    Shade $X \cap Y$.

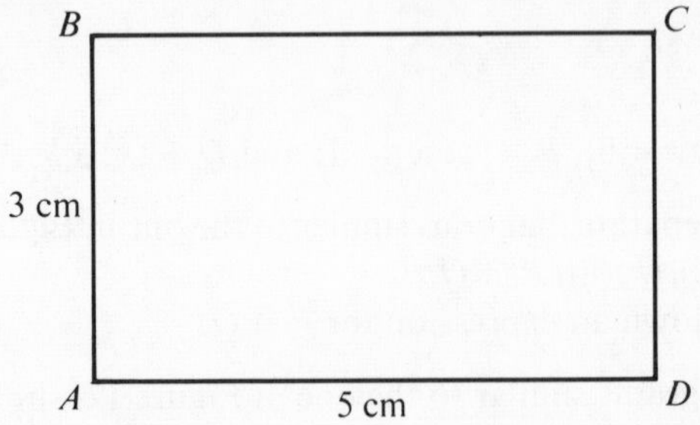

Fig. 14

14 (a) Construct the triangle ABC such that $AC = 6$ cm, $\angle A = 45°$ and $\angle B = 75°$.

    (b) If $\mathscr{E} = \{\text{points in the interior of triangle } ABC\}$, shade the locus $\{P: \angle PAC > \angle PCA\}$.

15 Draw a triangle ABC in which $AB > AC$. If $\mathscr{E} = \{\text{points in the interior of triangle } ABC\}$, $X = \{P: PB < PC\}$ and $Y = \{P: \angle PAC < \angle PAB\}$, construct the sets X and Y. What is $X \cap Y$?

16 Use set notation to describe each of the shaded regions in Figure 15. (A full line indicates that the boundary is included with the shaded region and a dotted line that it is excluded.)

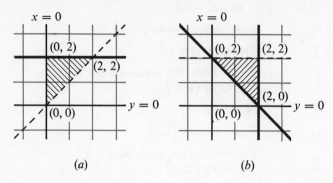

Fig. 15   (a)   (b)

Summary

Symbol	Meaning
$\{x: \ldots\}$	the set of objects x such that ...
$\mathscr{E}$	universal set
A'	complement of A
$\varnothing$	empty set
$\in$	is a member of
$\notin$	is not a member of
$n(A)$	number of members of A
$\subset$	is a subset of
$\supset$	contains
$A \cup B$	union of A and B
$A \cap B$	intersection of A and B

Abbreviation	Transformation	Inverse
X̰	Reflection in $y = 0$	
Y̰	Reflection in $x = 0$	
Q̰	Anticlockwise quarter-turn about $(0,0)$	
H̰	Half-turn about $(0,0)$	
T̰	Translation $\binom{4}{1}$	
Ḛ	Enlargement, scale factor 2, centre $(0,0)$	
Ḭ	Identity	
Ṵ	Translation $\binom{-4}{-1}$	
F̰	Enlargement, scale factor $\frac{1}{2}$, centre $(0,0)$	
J̰	Clockwise quarter-turn about $(0,0)$	
M̰	Reflection in $x = 4$	
V̰	Clockwise quarter-turn about $(4,1)$	
S̰	Shear with invariant line $y = 0$ taking $(0,1)$ to $(1,1)$	
L̰	Shear with invariant line $y = 0$ taking $(0,1)$ to $(-1,1)$	

4 Combination of transformations II

The table is a copy of the one you produced whilst working through Chapter 2. The abbreviations will be used again in this chapter.

1 Transformations in general

(a) We have already seen in Chapter 2 that the transformation **XY** has the same effect on geometrical figures as the transformations **YX** and **H**. That is, **XY** and **YX** are both equivalent to a half-turn about $(0,0)$ (see Figure 1).

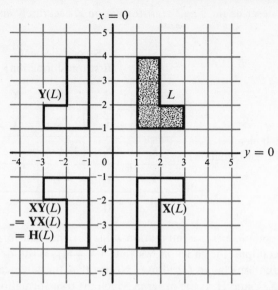

Fig. 1

When we are interested in the transformations we are dealing with, and not with the particular figures which are being transformed, we use letters in heavy type. We can write

$$\mathbf{XY} = \mathbf{YX} = \mathbf{H}$$

Make sure you understand the distinction between **XY**(*L*) and **XY** before you continue.

(*b*) The transformation **QX** has been applied to the triangle *T* in Figure 2. If **QX** = **K** describe the single transformation **K** accurately and add it to your list. (The broken line will help you with your answer.)

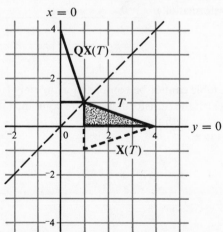

Fig. 2

(*c*) Copy Figure 2 and draw **XQ**(*T*). Is **QX** = **XQ**?

41

Combination of transformations II

If $XQ = Z$ describe the single transformation Z accurately and add it to your list.

(*d*)

	Second element (first transformation)			
	I	X	Y	H
I	I	X	Y	H
X	X	I		
Y	Y	H		
H	H			

First element (second transformation)

Copy and complete this combination table for the transformations **I, X, Y** and **H** (for example, the table shows that **YX = H**). Write down some transformation 'equations' as in (*a*) above. Notice that the table can be completed using only **I, X, Y** and **H**. Is the order in which the transformations are combined important?

(*e*) Study Figure 3 and use your answers to (*b*) and (*c*) to help you complete this transformation table:

	Second element (first transformation)			
	I	X	Y	Q
I				
X				
Y		H		
Q		K		

First element (second transformation)

Notice that this table cannot be completed using only **I, X, Y** and **Q**.

Is the order in which the transformations are combined important in this case? Compare your answers with those for (*d*).

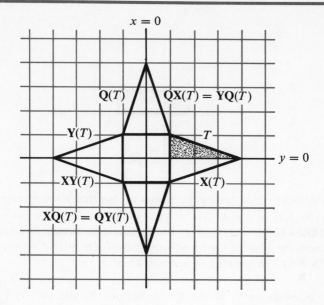

Fig. 3

Exercise A

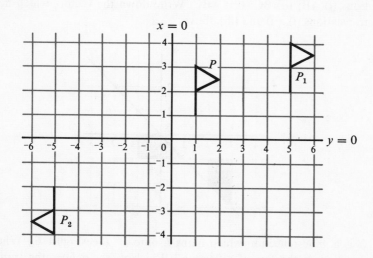

Fig. 4

1   In Figure 4 which transformations map (i) P onto P_1; (ii) P_1 onto P_2?
    What is the effect of the transformation **HT** applied to P? P can be mapped
    onto P_2 by two reflections. What are the equations of the lines of reflection?

Combination of transformations II

2

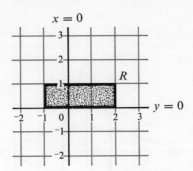

Fig. 5

S is a shear which leaves the points on the line $y = 0$ invariant and takes $(0,1)$ to $(1,1)$. **Z** is a shear which leaves the points on the line $x = 0$ invariant and takes $(1,0)$ to $(1,1)$. R is the rectangle in Figure 5. Draw a diagram to show the effect of the transformations (i) **ZS**; (ii) **SZ** on the rectangle R. Is **ZS** = **SZ**? What kind of figure is **ZS**(R)?

3 The translations **A**, **B** and **C** are defined by the vectors $\begin{pmatrix} 1 \\ 6 \end{pmatrix}, \begin{pmatrix} 2 \\ 2 \end{pmatrix}, \begin{pmatrix} -4 \\ 0 \end{pmatrix}$ respectively. Draw the images of the flag P in Figure 4 after the transformations (i) **AB**; (ii) **BC**; (iii) **ABC**. Write down the vectors which define the translations (i), (ii) and (iii) above.

4

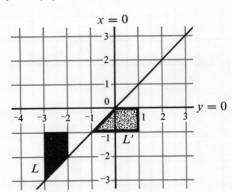

Fig. 6

G is a glide reflection which maps L onto L'. (See Figure 6.) What is the equation of the line of reflection? Which vector defines the translation? Draw the image $\mathbf{G}^2(L)$ ($\mathbf{G}^2$ is an abbreviation for **GG**) and describe the single transformation which maps L onto $\mathbf{G}^2(L)$.

5 **A** is a half-turn about $A(2,0)$. **B** is a half-turn about $B(4,^-1)$. Draw the images of P (the flag in Figure 4) after the transformations (i) **BA**; (ii) **AB**. Is **BA** = **AB**?

Which single transformations will map (i) **BA**(P) onto P; (ii) **AB**(P) onto P?

6   P is the point $(3,1)$.

   G is a glide-reflection made up of the translation $\begin{pmatrix} 2 \\ 0 \end{pmatrix}$ followed by a reflection in $y = 4$.

   M is a reflection in $x = 4$.

   Draw a diagram to show the positions of (i) **M**(P); (ii) **G**(P); (iii) **GM**(P); (iv) **MG**(P); (v) **G²**(P). What do your answers suggest about **MG** and **GM**?

7   Find single transformations from your list which are equivalent to (i) **EF**; (ii) **TU**; (iii) **J²**; (iv) **X³**; (v) **XYH**; (vi) **JQU**; (vii) **UQJ**.

8

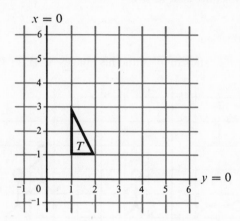

Fig. 7

A is an enlargement, scale factor 2, centre $(3,0)$.
E is defined on your list.

   Draw the image **AE**(T) where T is the triangle in Figure 7. What is the scale factor of enlargement for the transformation **AE**? Where is the centre of enlargement? Is **AE** = **EA**?

9   Using the pattern of Figure 3, Chapter 2, page 15, find examples to show that (i) two translations are equivalent to a single translation; (ii) two half-turns are equivalent to a translation; (iii) two reflections in parallel lines are equivalent to a translation; (iv) two reflections in perpendicular lines are equivalent to a half-turn. Tabulate your answers as below. Find at least two examples of each.

Object	1st image	Final image	1st transformation	2nd transformation	Single transformation
a	c	m	half-turn about $(0,0)$	half-turn about $(^-2, ^-1)$	translation $\begin{pmatrix} ^-4 \\ ^-2 \end{pmatrix}$

Combination of transformations II

10 Write down the transformation matrices defining (i) **H**; (ii) **E**.
    Premultiply the matrix for **E** by the matrix for **H**.
    Draw a diagram to help you find the single transformation equivalent to
    HE. Write down the matrix defining this single transformation. Explain
    your answers.

Summary

1 **AB** is the *combined transformation* first **B** and then **A**.

2 **AB** is not always equivalent to **BA**.

2 Inverse transformations

(*a*) Figure 8 shows a 'stick man' *A* and his images **X**(*A*), **T**(*A*), **M**(*A*) and **Q**(*A*).

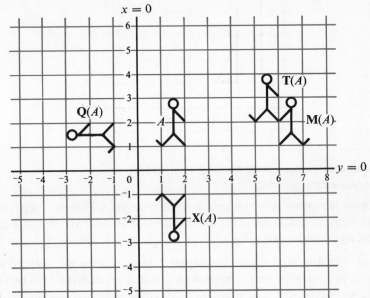

Fig. 8

X(*A*) can be mapped back onto *A* by a reflection in $y = 0$. Describe the transformations which map the other images back onto *A*.

(*b*) The transformations which map an image back onto the original object
are called *inverse* transformations.

We denote the inverse of transformation **B** in shorthand notation by **B**$^{-1}$.
Q^{-1}, the inverse of **Q**, is therefore a clockwise quarter-turn about $(0,0)$.

Describe the transformations **Y**$^{-1}$, **E**$^{-1}$, **J**$^{-1}$ and **V**$^{-1}$.

(*c*) Notice that **Q**$^{-1}$ = **J** and **X**$^{-1}$ = **X**. Let **V**$^{-1}$ = **P**, a quarter-turn about $(4, 1)$.
Now complete the 'Inverse' column on your list by entering **J** beside **Q**, **X** beside
X, **P** beside **V** and so on.

46

Check by looking at the transformations in your list that if **A** is the inverse of **B** then **B** is the inverse of **A**.

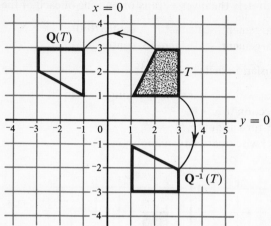

Fig. 9

(*d*) Figure 9 shows T, $\mathbf{Q}^{-1}(T)$ and $\mathbf{Q}(T)$. If we apply transformation $\mathbf{Q}^{-1}$ to $\mathbf{Q}(T)$ then obviously $\mathbf{Q}^{-1}\mathbf{Q}(T) = T$ by the definition of $\mathbf{Q}^{-1}$, and we can see that $\mathbf{Q}^{-1}\mathbf{Q} = \mathbf{I} = \mathbf{Q}\mathbf{Q}^{-1}$; i.e. $\mathbf{Q}^{-1}\mathbf{Q}$ and $\mathbf{Q}\mathbf{Q}^{-1}$ leave the positions of objects unchanged.

(*e*) Generally **A** is the inverse of **B** if

$$\mathbf{AB} = \mathbf{BA} = \mathbf{I}$$

and in this case we can write

$$\mathbf{A} = \mathbf{B}^{-1}$$

and

$$\mathbf{B} = \mathbf{A}^{-1}.$$

(*f*) Some transformations are their own inverses. We say they are self-inverse. For example:

a reflection in $y = 0$ followed by a reflection in $y = 0$ will map any object back onto itself, so that

$$\mathbf{X}^2 = \mathbf{I}, \text{ and } \mathbf{X} = \mathbf{X}^{-1} \quad \text{(see Figure 10).}$$

Which transformations in your list are self-inverse?

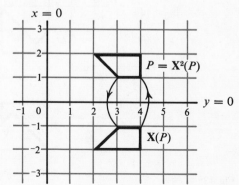

Fig. 10

47

Combination of transformations II

Exercise B

1 Describe accurately the inverse transformations of each of the following:

    (i) enlargement, scale factor 2, centre $(0,0)$;

    (ii) enlargement, scale factor 3, centre $(2,5)$;

    (iii) translation defined by $\begin{pmatrix} 9 \\ -7 \end{pmatrix}$;

    (iv) shear with $y = 0$ invariant taking $(0,1)$ to $(1,1)$;

    (v) reflection in $x = 8$;

    (vi) half-turn about (a,b);

    (vii) clockwise quarter-turn about $(6, {}^-1)$.

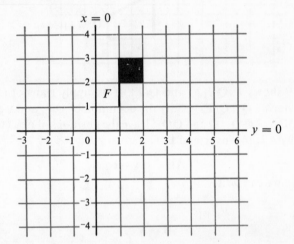

Fig. 11

2 **A** is a half-turn about $(2,0)$; **B** is a reflection in $x = 3$; **C** is a clockwise quarter-turn about $(1,1)$. Draw the following images of flag F in Figure 11: (i) $\mathbf{A}^{-1}(F)$; (ii) $\mathbf{B}^{-1}(F)$; (iii) $\mathbf{C}^{-1}(F)$; (iv) $\mathbf{C}^{-1}\mathbf{A}^{-1}(F)$.

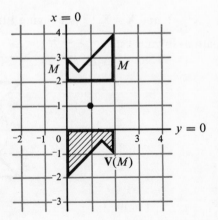

Fig. 12

48

3   In Figure 12 the shape M has been given a half-turn about $(1,1)$ to $\mathbf{V}(M)$. Describe $\mathbf{V}^{-1}$ in words. Is $\mathbf{V}^{-1}(M) = \mathbf{V}(M)$? If $\mathbf{V}(M)$ is now given a half-turn about $(2,0)$ to $\mathbf{DV}(M)$, describe simple transformations equivalent to (i) $\mathbf{DV}$; (ii) $(\mathbf{DV})^{-1}$.

4   Write down the coordinates of the points onto which $(0,0)$ is mapped by the transformations (i) $\mathbf{U}^{-1}$; (ii) $\mathbf{V}^{-1}$; (iii) $\mathbf{U}^{-1}\mathbf{V}^{-1}$; (iv) $\mathbf{UV}$; (v) $(\mathbf{UV})^{-1}$; (vi) $\mathbf{K}$; (vii) $\mathbf{K}^{-1}$; (viii) $\mathbf{K}^{-2}$.

5   $\mathbf{G}$ is the glide-reflection $\mathbf{XN}$ where $\mathbf{N}$ is a translation $\begin{pmatrix} 4 \\ 0 \end{pmatrix}$.

   Draw a diagram to show the effect of (i) $\mathbf{G}$; (ii) $\mathbf{G}^{-1}$ on a shape of your own choice. Is the statement $\mathbf{G}^{-1} = (\mathbf{XN})^{-1} = \mathbf{X}^{-1}\mathbf{N}^{-1} = \mathbf{N}^{-1}\mathbf{X}^{-1}$ a completely true statement?

6   Simplify $(\mathbf{A}^{-1})^{-1}$.

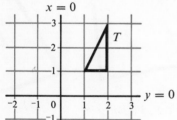

Fig. 13

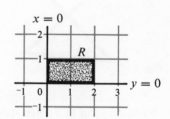

Fig. 14

7   Copy Figure 13 and draw the images $\mathbf{QX}(T)$; $(\mathbf{QX})^{-1}(T)$; $\mathbf{Q}^{-1}\mathbf{X}^{-1}(T)$ and $\mathbf{X}^{-1}\mathbf{Q}^{-1}(T)$. Is $(\mathbf{QX})^{-1} = \mathbf{Q}^{-1}\mathbf{X}^{-1}$? Is $\mathbf{Q}^{-1}\mathbf{X}^{-1} = \mathbf{X}^{-1}\mathbf{Q}^{-1}$?

8   Describe in words the transformation $\mathbf{S}^{-1}$. Copy Figure 14 and draw a diagram to show $\mathbf{XS}(R)$. Describe in words the transformation $(\mathbf{XS})^{-1}$. Draw a diagram to show $(\mathbf{XS})^{-1}(R)$. Is $\mathbf{X}^{-1}\mathbf{S}^{-1} = (\mathbf{XS})^{-1}$?

Summary

1   The inverse of $\mathbf{A}$ is the transformation which maps $\mathbf{A}(G)$, where G is any object, back onto G. The inverse is written $\mathbf{A}^{-1}$.

2   If $\mathbf{AB} = \mathbf{BA} = \mathbf{I}$ then $\mathbf{B} = \mathbf{A}^{-1}$ and $\mathbf{A} = \mathbf{B}^{-1}$.

Four-sided shapes

(*a*) How would you describe the shapes in Figure 1?

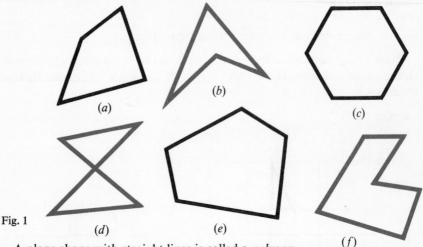

Fig. 1

A plane shape with straight lines is called a *polygon*.

The polygon in Figure 1(*a*) is *convex*. Which of the other shapes in Figure 1 are convex?

Explain with the aid of a diagram why the polygon in Figure 1(*b*) is not convex.

(*b*) Draw a convex quadrilateral with rotational symmetry of order 2, that is, draw a convex quadrilateral which can be mapped onto itself by a half-turn.

Where is the centre of the rotational symmetry?

Are both pairs of opposite sides of your quadrilateral parallel?

Is it possible to draw a quadrilateral which has rotational symmetry of order 2 but which does not have both pairs of opposite sides parallel?

A *convex* quadrilateral with rotational symmetry of order 2 is called a parallelogram.

Rotational symmetry of order 2 is sometimes called *point symmetry*.

(*c*) Figure 2 shows some special parallelograms. They are special because they have some additional symmetries.

Copy these parallelograms on to squared paper and draw any lines of symmetry which they possess.

You should find that the parallelogram in Figure 2(*b*) has two lines of symmetry which are the mediators of the sides. How would you describe the lines of symmetry possessed by the other two parallelograms?

What are the names of these special parallelograms?

How many different transformations map each of these shapes onto itself?

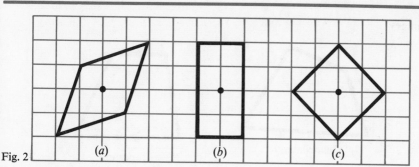

Fig. 2   (a)   (b)   (c)

(*d*) Since rhombuses, rectangles and squares have rotational symmetry of order 2, they are parallelograms. Therefore if

$$P = \{\text{parallelograms}\},$$
$$H = \{\text{rhombuses}\},$$
$$R = \{\text{rectangles}\}$$
and
$$S = \{\text{squares}\},$$

we can write the inclusion relations:

$$H \subset P, \ R \subset P \text{ and } S \subset P$$
or:
$$P \supset H, \ P \supset R \text{ and } P \supset S.$$

What do the symbols $\subset$ and $\supset$ mean?

Does a square have all the symmetries of a rhombus? Does it have other symmetries as well?

Is it true that (i) $S \subset H$; (ii) $H \supset S$?

Write down a relation which connects S and R.

(*e*) Draw a quadrilateral which has the symmetries of both a rhombus and a rectangle. What kind of quadrilateral have you drawn? What can you say about $R \cap H$?

(*f*) Draw a convex quadrilateral with *exactly one* line of symmetry which is a mediator of a pair of sides. What name do we give to this type of quadrilateral?

Do all trapeziums have line symmetry?

Now draw (i) a convex quadrilateral, (ii) a non-convex quadrilateral, with exactly one line of symmetry which is a bisector of a pair of angles. What names do we give to these types of quadrilateral? If you do not know a name, suggest one.

If
$$H = \{\text{rhombuses}\},$$
$$I = \{\text{isosceles trapeziums}\},$$
$$K = \{\text{kites}\}$$
and
$$T = \{\text{trapeziums}\},$$

which of the following relations are true: (i) $I \subset T$; (ii) $T \supset I$; (iii) $H \subset I$; (iv) $H \subset T$; (v) $T \subset K$; (vi) $K \supset H$?

Four-sided shapes

Summary

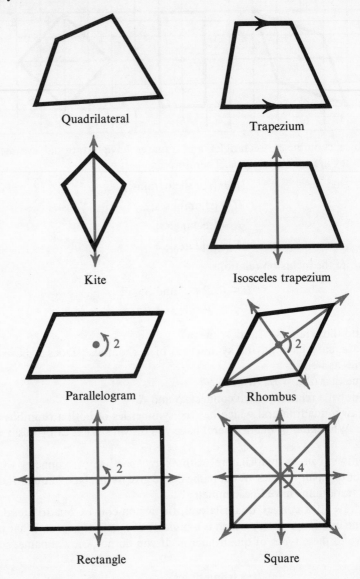

Fig. 3. *Convex quadrilaterals*

Exercise A

1 Name two types of quadrilateral which have two, and only two, lines of symmetry.

2 If $\mathscr{E}$ = {quadrilaterals}, P = {quadrilaterals with point symmetry} and Q = {quadrilaterals with line symmetry}, draw and name a quadrilateral which is a member of:

  (a) $P' \cap Q$;
  (b) $P \cap Q'$;
  (c) $P \cap Q$;
  (d) $P' \cap Q'$.

3 State which of the following shapes always has at least one line of symmetry: (i) a parallelogram; (ii) a kite; (iii) a trapezium with no two sides equal.

4 Is it possible to draw a quadrilateral with rotational symmetry of

  (a) order 1;
  (b) order 2;
  (c) order 3;
  (d) order 4;
  (e) order 8?

5 If $\mathscr{E}$ = {quadrilaterals}, P = {parallelograms}, R = {rectangles} and H = {rhombuses}, draw a diagram to show how these sets are related.

6

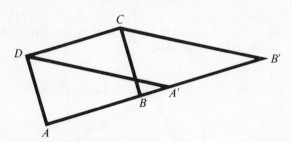

Fig. 4

The rectangle $ABCD$ is sheared into the position $A'B'CD$. Say what symmetry, if any, the shape $A'B'CD$ has.

7 If P = {parallelograms} and Q = {quadrilaterals whose opposite angles add to 180°}, describe $P \cap Q$ as simply as possible.

8 (a) Which of the following shapes always have half-turn symmetry about the point of intersection of the diagonals: (i) a rhombus; (ii) a rectangle; (iii) a trapezium; (iv) a kite?
  (b) Which of the above shapes always have line symmetry about both diagonals?

9 Q is a set of quadrilaterals each of which has p lines of symmetry.

  (a) State all possible values of p.
  (b) Name the type of quadrilateral for which $p > 3$.

10 $S = \{\text{squares}\}$, $K = \{\text{kites}\}$, $P = \{\text{parallelograms}\}$ and $R = \{\text{rhombuses}\}$.

    (*a*) Write down all the inclusion relations between the sets S, K, P and R.

    (*b*) Draw a *single* diagram to show these inclusion relations.

    (*c*) Make clearly labelled sketches of possible quadrilaterals x, y and z such that $x \in K \cap R'$, $y \in P \cap R'$ and $z \in P \cap K$, showing all the axes and centres of symmetry.

11 Two rods of length 13 cm and two of length 5 cm are joined at their ends to form a convex quadrilateral which may be either a kite or a parallelogram. The diagonals are of length D cm and d cm, D being greater than d.

    Copy and complete, for each case, the inequalities satisfied by D and d.

    (*a*) *Kite* $< D <$
                                     $< d <$

    (*b*) *Parallelogram* $< D <$
                                       $< d <$

12 In Figure 5, $ABCD$ is a square and lengths are as shown. $\mathbf{Q}$ represents a clockwise quarter-turn about the centre of $ABCD$.

    (*a*) State the image under $\mathbf{Q}$ of (i) A, (ii) AE.

    (*b*) State the image of E under (i) $\mathbf{Q}^2$, (ii) $\mathbf{Q}^3$, (iii) $\mathbf{Q}^4$.

    (*c*) Is $EFGH$ a square? State one or more properties of a square which justify your conclusion.

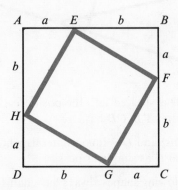

Fig. 5

13 All quadrilaterals which are members of the set R have property D. Is it necessarily true that quadrilaterals which have property D are members of the set R?

    Give an example to illustrate your answer.

14 A, B, C and D are four statements which may be either true or false and which are connected by the relation $\Rightarrow$ as shown in Figure 6.

    $A \Rightarrow B$ means 'if A is true, then B is also true'.

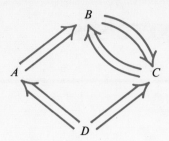

Fig. 6

(a) If *A* is true, which other statements *must* be true?
(b) Which statement is such that its truth implies the truth of the other three statements?
(c) Copy the following statements and label them *A*, *B*, *C* and *D* so that all implications of the diagram apply to them:

'The quadrilateral *Q* has both pairs of opposite sides equal'.
'*Q* is a square'.
'*Q* is a parallelogram'.
'*Q* has all four sides equal'.

Revision exercises

Calculate the following, giving all answers as accurately as your slide rule permits:

1	$943 \div 0 \cdot 026$.	2	41×650.	3	$2 \cdot 43 \times 16 \cdot 2$.
4	$374 \div 12 \cdot 7$.	5	$\dfrac{1 \cdot 82 \times 0 \cdot 64}{52 \cdot 7}$.	6	$\sqrt{57 \cdot 2}$.
7	$(3 \cdot 95)^2$.	8	$\sqrt{4 \cdot 25}$.	9	$(0 \cdot 24)^3$.
10	$\sqrt[3]{780}$.				

Slide rule session no. 2

Calculate the following, giving all answers as accurately as you can:

1	$(0 \cdot 0155)^2$.	2	$22 \cdot 5 \times 19 \cdot 6$.	3	$0 \cdot 159 \div 0 \cdot 0725$.
4	$1 \cdot 64 \times 12 \cdot 6$.	5	$705 \times 0 \cdot 0915$.	6	$3 \cdot 05 \div 695$.
7	$158 \cdot 5 \div 0 \cdot 124$.	8	$(43 \cdot 5)^2$.	9	$\sqrt{(43 \cdot 5)}$.
10	$\pi \times (3 \cdot 6)^2$.				

Quick quiz no. 1

1 Calculate 6×7 in base eight.
2 How many square centimetres are there in 1 m^2?
3 Give the next term of the sequence $1, 1, 2, 3, 5, 8, \ldots$.
4 Calculate $119 \times 57 - 117 \times 57$.
5 Find the value of $p(q + r)$ when $p = 3$, $q = {}^-2$ and $r = {}^-1$.
6 Write down the value of $\sqrt{1 \cdot 21}$.
7 Add 111_2 and 1011_2, giving the answer in binary form.
8 Carry out the matrix multiplication

$$\begin{pmatrix} 1 & 2 \\ -3 & 0 \end{pmatrix} \begin{pmatrix} 4 & 5 \\ 6 & 7 \end{pmatrix}.$$

9 One angle of an isosceles triangle is $136°$. Find the other angles.
10 Calculate $15 \times 10 \times 5 \times 0$.

Quick quiz no. 2

1 Calculate $0 \cdot 1 \times 0 \cdot 01$.
2 Find the cost of 26 litres of petrol at 8p per litre.

3 What is the probability that when a coin is tossed twice it will come down heads twice in succession?

4 Calculate $\frac{5}{12} - \frac{2}{15}$, giving the answer as a fraction in its simplest terms.

5 Find the area of a triangle whose base is 17 cm and whose height is 10 cm.

6 $(2.88 \div 1.2) \div 0.6$.

7 What is the image of the point $(5, 5)$ after reflection in the line $y = x$?

8 Give the number-base of the correct addition $27 + 6 = 34$.

9 A regular polygon has exterior angles of $20°$. How many sides has it?

10 What is 12% of 175?

Exercise A

1 If $n(X \cup Y) = 25$, $n(X \cap Y) = 5$ and $n(Y) = 14$, draw a Venn diagram to illustrate these data, and find $n(X)$.

2 Solve the following equations:

  (a) $2x + 4 = 10$;   (b) $2x - 4 = 10$.

3 Eight boys are comparing how much pocket money they have received that week, and they find that each has 50p. A ninth boy joins the group who has been given £5 (his father has won a football pool!). Calculate the mean and median pocket money before and after the ninth boy joined the group.

4

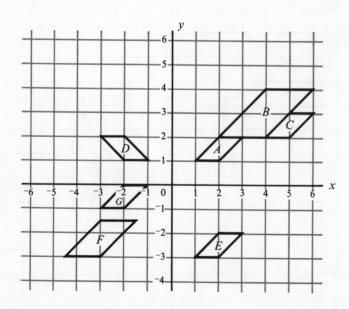

Fig. 1

In Figure 1, starting with parallelogram A, how can each of the others be obtained from A? State the transformations.

5 Calculate the following matrix products where possible:

(a) $(1 \quad 2)\begin{pmatrix} 1 \\ -2 \end{pmatrix};$ (b) $(1 \quad 2)\begin{pmatrix} 1 & 3 \\ -2 & 4 \end{pmatrix};$

(c) $(1 \quad 2 \quad 0)\begin{pmatrix} 1 & 3 \\ -2 & 4 \end{pmatrix};$ (d) $\begin{pmatrix} 1 & 3 & 0 \\ 2 & -4 & 6 \end{pmatrix}\begin{pmatrix} -5 \\ 1 \end{pmatrix};$

(e) $\begin{pmatrix} 0 & 1 \\ 0 & 6 \end{pmatrix}\begin{pmatrix} 1 & -3 \\ 0 & 0 \end{pmatrix};$ (f) $\begin{pmatrix} 0 & 1 \\ 0 & 6 \end{pmatrix}(1 \quad 2 \quad 3).$

Exercise B

1 The numbers of the principal farm animals in Great Britain are (to a sufficient degree of accuracy): sheep 30 million, cattle 12 million, pigs 6 million. A pie chart is to be drawn to illustrate the proportions of the three kinds of animal. State the angle of the sector which represents pigs.

2 If $\mathbf{A} = \begin{pmatrix} 1 & 2 \\ 3 & 4 \end{pmatrix}$, $\mathbf{B} = \begin{pmatrix} -1 & 0 \\ -2 & 3 \end{pmatrix}$, $\mathbf{C} = \begin{pmatrix} 3 & -2 \\ 2 & -4 \end{pmatrix}$, find the following matrices:

(a) $\mathbf{A} + \mathbf{B};$ (b) $\mathbf{B} + \mathbf{C};$ (c) $\mathbf{A} + \mathbf{C};$ (d) $\mathbf{A} - \mathbf{B};$

(e) $3\mathbf{C};$ (f) $4\mathbf{A};$ (g) $3\mathbf{C} + 4\mathbf{A};$ (h) $3\mathbf{C} - \mathbf{A};$

(i) $\mathbf{C} - \mathbf{B} - \mathbf{A};$ (j) $3\mathbf{C} + 4\mathbf{A} - 2\mathbf{B}.$

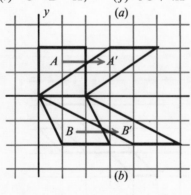

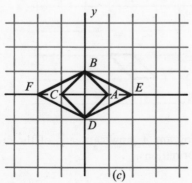

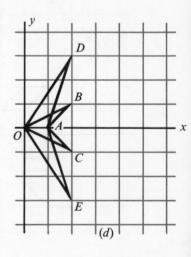

Fig. 2

58

3   (a) In Figure 2(a) what geometrical transformation maps the figure A onto A'?

(b) What geometrical transformation maps the figure B onto B' in Figure 2(b)?

(c) In Figure 2(c), ABCD has been transformed onto EBFD. What geometrical transformation has been performed?

(d) In Figure 2(d), ODAE is the image of OBAC. What geometrical transformation has been performed?

4   Is it always, sometimes or never true that $(X \cap Y) \subset (X \cup Y)$?

5   (a) Let $M = \begin{pmatrix} 1 & -2 \\ 3 & 1 \end{pmatrix}$ and $N = \begin{pmatrix} 2 & 1 \\ 0 & 1 \end{pmatrix}$. Find MN and NM. Are they equal?

(b) ABCD is a parallelogram. If the coordinates of A, B, C are (0,0), (2,1) and (3,3) respectively, what are the coordinates of D?

5 Computation

1 A reminder

When we say that the answer to a problem is 4·61 correct to 2 D.P. (decimal places) we mean that the answer is nearer 4·61 than it is to 4·60 or 4·62, i.e.

$$4\cdot605 \leqslant \text{true answer} < 4\cdot615.$$

Notice that the inequality sign on the right hand does not include equality. This is because by convention we always 'round up' when the last figure we consider is 5. For example, if the result of our calculation was 4·605 and we wanted this correct to 2 D.P. we would write the answer as 4·61.

Exercise A

Write each of the following exact results to (i) 2 D.P.; (ii) 1 D.P.

    (a) 4·616;   (b) 4·614;   (c) 0·045;   (d) 0·555;   (e) 6·040.

2 Significant figures and estimating

(a) The number of spectators at a Manchester United v. Derby County football match was 45 191.

A television commentator told the viewers that 45 000 people had watched the match. He was not lying! All he was interested in doing was informing the viewers of the number of spectators correct to the nearest 1000. To him, and to most of the viewers, the remaining figures are not very significant. He was stating the number correct to 2 significant figures (2 S.F.).

Here are some more attendance figures for the same Saturday. If you were a commentator, how many people would you say attended each game? To how many significant figures are you stating your answers?

Huddersfield *v.* Manchester City   21 922
Barnsley *v.* Mansfield   2061

(*b*) To give the numbers for the Manchester United game correct to 1 S.F. we would write 50 000. This is correct to the nearest 10 000. It is the figure on the left of a number which is the most significant and the figure on the right which is the least significant.

Correct the numbers in Exercise A to 1 S.F. Discuss why we ignore the '0's in (*c*) and (*d*) but not in (*e*) in counting the significant figures.

(*c*) The numbers in Exercise A to 2 S.F. are (*a*) 4·6; (*b*) 4·6; (*c*) 0·045 (why are we able to give an answer when we can only see 2 significant figures in this case?); (*d*) 0·56; (*e*) 6·0.

These should help you to answer (*b*) above if you are not certain of your results.

The first non-zero figure counting from the left is the first significant figure. All the zeros after this are significant.

We use significant figures in estimating amounts or numbers, and when we are doing rough calculations.

(*d*) Estimate the number of dots in Figure 1. Explain how you arrived at your answer. To how many significant figures do you think your answer is correct?

Fig. 1

(*e*) The number of dots in Figure 1 is 234. There are several ways of estimating the number. One way is to assume that the number of dots in each row is constant, to count the dots in the first row (say) and to multiply by 10 (the number of rows). This gives an answer $23 \times 10 = 230$ which is quite a good estimate and is correct to 2 S.F.

Using the method above what is the 'worst' estimate that could be made? Now estimate the number of letters on this page.

(*f*) We make estimates to help us to make decisions. In some cases estimates need to be very reliable (for example in considering the amount of blood required to be kept in blood banks at a hospital for emergency cases). In others they are not so important and are meant to give us a rough guideline. Read through the following examples before you attempt Exercise B.

Example 1

If you were in charge of ordering programmes for Manchester United's next home match, how many programmes would you order?

First of all we really need more information about crowd numbers expected at Manchester. We should also take into account the attraction of the opposing team, and the fraction of the crowd that usually buys programmes.

If we only have the information from section (*a*) we might assume that the crowd will be 45 000 (to 2 s.f.). Let us also assume that $\frac{1}{4}$ of the spectators usually buy programmes. $\frac{1}{4}$ of 45 000 is 10 000 (to 1 s.f.) so $\frac{3}{4}$ is 30 000. How accurate is this?

Example 2

A lorry is loaded and found to hold 5120 bricks. There are 20 000 bricks to be moved altogether. How many lorry loads is this?

Clearly in this problem the 120 bricks is not important, so we divide 20 000 by 5000 to obtain 4.

Exercise B

1 To how many significant figures are each of the following stated?

    (i) The distance from Reading to London is 54 km;
    (ii) 1 mile $\approx 1\cdot609$ km ($\approx$ means 'approximately equal to');
    (iii) the time for a hundred metres race was $10\cdot0$ s.

2 Correct each of the following (*a*) to 3 s.f.; (*b*) to 3 d.p.

    (i) $3\cdot6846$;   (ii) $0\cdot004614$;   (iii) $467\cdot0467$.

Discuss whether giving an answer to a given number of s.f. gives a 'better' approximation than an answer to the same number of d.p. What is the general rule?

3 Correct each of the following to 1 s.f.

    (i) $8\cdot76$;   (ii) $0\cdot495$;   (iii) $17\cdot8$.

Hence find approximate answers for:

    (*a*) $8\cdot76 \times 0\cdot495 \times 17\cdot8$;   (*b*) $(8\cdot76 + 0\cdot495) \times 17\cdot8$;

    (*c*) $\dfrac{8\cdot76 \times 0\cdot495}{17\cdot8}$.

4   Carry out rough calculations to see whether the following results (which have been done on a slide rule) are approximately correct:

   (i) $275 \times 992 = 27\,280$;   (vi) $3140 \times 2 \cdot 95 = 926$;
   (ii) $8806 \times 0 \cdot 845 = 744$;   (vii) $0 \cdot 914 \times 0 \cdot 73 = 0 \cdot 667$;
   (iii) $67 \cdot 4 \times 0 \cdot 0012 = 8 \cdot 09$;   (viii) $98\,534 \div 62 \cdot 7 = 1570$;
   (iv) $25 \cdot 04 \div 0 \cdot 46 = 5 \cdot 44$;   (ix) $0 \cdot 006\,43 \div 5 \cdot 81 = 0 \cdot 001\,108$;
   (v) $375 \times 569 \div 42 \cdot 3 = 0 \cdot 061$;   (x) $3 \cdot 142 \div 61 \cdot 3 = 0 \cdot 523$.

5   Estimate how much it would cost to buy one of these text books for every pupil in the school.

6   To how many S.F. are the values in your SMP Tables given? Is the number of S.F. constant within each table?

7   Answer Question 6 replacing S.F. by D.P. What do we mean by 3-figure tables?

8   1 kg $\approx$ 2·20 lb to 3 S.F. Estimate the total weight in kg of the members of your class. To how many S.F. do you think your answer is correct?

9   You wish to paint two ceilings measuring 6·4 m $\times$ 4·6 m and 10·8 m $\times$ 6·7 m. Each tin of paint is said to cover 12 m² and costs 93p. Estimate the number of tins of paint you should buy. How much do you think the job will cost?

10   If it is summer, estimate the number of runs scored in the first class cricket matches last Saturday. If it is winter, estimate the number of people who watched First Division football matches.

11   Estimate the total area of paper in cm² used to produce this book.

12   (You will need to do some research before you can give answers to this question.) Estimate:

   (i) the number of litres of petrol needed to drive to Barcelona and back in a Mini;
   (ii) the average height in cm you grow each year;
   (iii) the cost per year of providing every school child in England with free lunches.

3   Approximations

(a) Calculate the following exactly: (i) $2 \cdot 7 \times 3 \cdot 1$; (ii) $0 \cdot 46 + 0 \cdot 419$; (iii) $0 \cdot 25 \div 1 \cdot 25$; (iv) $1\frac{1}{2} \times 1\frac{3}{4}$; (v) the area of a square of side 11·2 cm.

(b) Measure the length of the line segment AB in Figure 2 with a ruler and check your answer with others in your class.

Fig. 2 A |————————————————————| B

Whose answer is correct?
Do you think anyone managed to measure AB *exactly*?

(c) Here are two possible answers for the length of *AB*:

    (i) 6·4 cm (to 1 D.P.);

    (ii) 6 cm (to 1 S.F.).

None of the answers are exact, but each is equally correct. What is important is that the *degree of accuracy* has been stated, i.e.

    (i) is correct to the nearest mm;

    (ii) is correct to the nearest cm.

Can you find a better approximation to the length of *AB* using your ruler? You will probably need a magnifying glass and your eyesight will have to be very good! Even then it will be very difficult to state the answer to 2 D.P. with any certainty.

(d) All measurements, no matter how sophisticated the measuring instruments, are always approximate. Some instruments, of course, are capable of giving 'better' approximations than others. For example, a micrometer would give a better approximation to the true diameter of a smooth piece of tubing than would a ruler or a tape measure.

What do you think would give the better approximation to the weight of your pen, a beam balance or a spring balance? Find out the degree of accuracy the balances in your science department will give.

(e) When we say then that the length of *AB* is 6·4 cm (to 1 D.P.) we mean that the length is nearer to 6·4 cm than it is to 6·35 cm or 6·45 cm, i.e.

$$6{\cdot}35 \leqslant AB < 6{\cdot}45.$$

What do we mean when we say that the length is 6 cm (to 1 S.F.)?

This means that whenever we measure there is an error involved.

The maximum error in measuring *AB* as 6·4 cm is 0·05 cm. What is the maximum error involved in measuring *AB* as 6 cm?

Exercise C

1   Use your ruler to measure the length of the rod in Figure 3 correct to (i) 1 D.P.; (ii) the nearest cm; (iii) 2 S.F. Which answer gives the best approximation?

Fig. 3

2   Give an example of a measurement that could be reasonably given as 10 cm and another that could be given as 10·3 cm.

3   Write the answers you obtained to the questions in section (a) correct to (i) 2 D.P.; (ii) 2 S.F.

4   Why do you think it is more accurate to use a pair of dividers and a ruler to measure lengths than to use only a ruler?

5   $\sqrt{5} \approx 2$. Find a better approximation correct to 1 D.P.

6   I measured the length of my garden as 11 m (to 2 S.F.). What is (i) the maximum length my garden could be; (ii) the minimum length it could be? What is the maximum error in measuring my garden as 11 m (to 2 S.F.)?

7   Scientists need very small units to measure the distance between atoms. They use the Angstrom (Å) as the unit, where 100 000 000 Å = 1 cm. What is the maximum error in measuring the distance between two atoms as (a) 2 Å; (b) 4·5 Å? Express each of these maximum errors in cm.

8   Distances between stars are measured in 'light years'. A light year is the distance a ray of light will travel in one year, and the speed of light is approximately 310 000 km/s. What is the maximum error involved in measuring the distance of a planet from the earth as 3·7 light years?
   Estimate the distance in km of a planet 2 light years away from earth.

9   A wooden rod is measured as 4 m (to 1 S.F.) and another as 5 m (to 1 S.F.). Discuss whether or not it is true to say that the total length of the rods is 9 m (to 1 S.F.).

10 Measure the width of your desk in metres to (a) 1 D.P.; (b) 2 D.P. A classroom is 8 m wide. Which of your answers would you use to find how many rows of desks can reasonably be arranged in the room, with the outer desks against the walls and with gangways at least 0·5 m wide?

11 Find the area of the shape in Figure 4 in cm² by tracing it onto graph paper and counting the squares. Explain how you could obtain a better approximation.

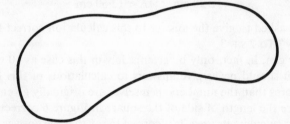

Fig. 4

4   Limits of accuracy

(a) We have already seen that any measurement is only approximate and can only be as accurate as the instrument used to make it. When we do not know an exact answer, however, we can often state the limits within which it must lie in the form

lower limit ≤ true answer ≤ upper limit.

For example, if my height lies between 1·80 m and 1·90 m, I can write

1·80 m ≤ my height ≤ 1·90 m

Computation

or, alternatively

$$\text{my height} = 1.85 \text{ m} \pm 5 \text{ cm}.$$

Write down your own height in these ways.

(*b*) Measure the length of the line segments *AB*, *BC*, *CD* and *DE* in Figure 5 to the nearest mm. Write down the limits within which the lengths lie. You should find the lengths are each 3·1 cm (to 1 D.P.).

If you now say that the total length of the line segment *AE* is 4×3.1 cm = 12·4 cm to the nearest cm, are you correct?

Measure *AE* and check your answer.

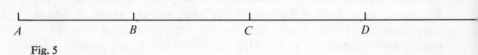

A   B   C   D

Fig. 5

(*c*) You should have found the measured length to be 12·5 cm (to 1 D.P.). Can you explain what went wrong with the calculation?

(*d*) In fact the length of each line segment is a little more than 3·1 cm, so that when we add these 'extra' bits four times we get an 'extra' 0·1 cm on the actual measurement, which is lost in the calculation. You can see from this that we must be very careful when we are making calculations from initial approximations.

(*e*) Whenever calculations are made with numbers of limited accuracy we must remember that there will be possible errors in the answers. What can be said with certainty about the length *AE* is that it is less than 4×3.15 cm and greater than 4×3.05 cm, i.e.

$$12.20 \text{ cm} \leqslant AE < 12.60 \text{ cm}.$$

If you were asked to give the answer to this calculation correct to 3 s.f. what would you say? To 2 s.f.?

The answer can, in fact, only be given safely in this case as 10 cm (to 1 s.f.). In general you should never give answers to calculations of this kind to more significant figures than the numbers themselves are originally given.

(*f*) Measure the length of side of the square in Figure 6 correct to 2 s.f. Use your answer to calculate its area. Is it correct to say that the answer is 11·56 cm²? To how many significant figures can you safely give your answer?

Fig. 6

Example 3

The time for one full swing of a pendulum is 4·3 s (to 2 s.f.). How many full swings will the pendulum make in 43 s?

At first glance it seems that the answer should be 10. However, the time of swing (t) lies within the following limits:

$$4·25 \text{ s} \leqslant t < 4·35 \text{ s}.$$

A quick calculation will tell you that if it is swinging in 4·35 s then 9 full swings take 39·15 s and 10 full swings take 43·5 s.

If it is swinging in 4·25 s then 10 full swings take 42·5 s and 11 full swings 46·75 s. The correct answer is therefore 9 or 10 full swings.

Example 4

The length of side (l) of a square is 3·6 cm (to 2 s.f.). What can you say about the true area (A) of the square?

We know that

$$3·55 \text{ cm} \leqslant l < 3·65 \text{ cm}.$$

and therefore that

$$(3·55)^2 \text{ cm}^2 \leqslant A < (3·65)^2 \text{ cm}^2$$
$$12·6025 \text{ cm}^2 \leqslant A < 13·3325 \text{ cm}^2.$$

We can say that the area of the square lies between those two limits and that it is 13 cm² (to 2 s.f.). Check this with your answer to (f) above, because you should have measured the length of the square as 3·6 cm.

Exercise D

1   A baby has 8 coloured cubes which fit snugly into a cubic box. Each cube has 6·5 cm edges (to 2 s.f.). What is the least length the sides of the box could have? What is the least area the base of the box could have?

2   A rectangle has sides measured as 3·2 cm × 6·7 cm (each to 2 s.f.). What is the greatest perimeter the rectangle could have? What is the smallest possible perimeter?

3   My watch is subject to a possible error of 5 min and it takes me 12 min ± 3 min to get to school.

   (*a*) At what time, by my watch, must I leave in the morning to ensure that I get to school by 8.40 a.m.?

   (*b*) What is the earliest I am likely to reach school if I set off at 8.00 a.m. by my watch?

Computation

4   The number 15 bus takes 55 min ± 5 min for a complete journey. How many journeys would you expect it to make in an 8 hour day, if $1\frac{1}{2}$ hours are taken by breaks? Using your answer, find how long a rest the bus driver can expect at the end of each journey. Express your answer as:

$$\text{lower limit} \leqslant \text{rest time} \leqslant \text{upper limit.}$$

5   A lathe worker making precision instruments is told that the diameter of a piston he is making is to be 6·7 cm with 0·01 cm tolerance. What do you understand by this statement?

6   Use your slide rule to calculate 3·11 × 0·69. How accurate do you think your answer is? Calculate the exact answer and hence find the error you made.

5   Index form for numbers

(a) Copy and complete this number pattern:

$$
\begin{aligned}
10 \times 10 \times 10 \times 10 \times 10 &= 100\ 000\!\cdot\!0 & &= 10^5 \\
10 \times 10 \times 10 \times 10 &=\ 10\ 000\!\cdot\!0 & &= \\
&=\ \ \ 1000\!\cdot\!0 & &= 10^3 \\
10 \times 10 &= & &= 10^2 \\
10 &=\ \ \ \ \ \ 10\!\cdot\!0 & &= 10^1 \\
1 &=\ \ \ \ \ \ \ 1\!\cdot\!0 & &= \\
1/10 &=\ \ \ \ \ \ \ 0\!\cdot\!1 & &= 10^{-1} \\
1/(10 \times 10) &=\ \ \ \ \ \ 0\!\cdot\!01 & &= \\
1/(10 \times 10 \times 10) &=\ \ \ \ \ 0\!\cdot\!001 & &= 10^{-3} \\
&=\ \ \ \ 0\!\cdot\!0001 & &= 10^{-4} \\
1/(10 \times 10 \times 10 \times 10 \times 10) &= & &= 10^{-5}
\end{aligned}
$$

Notice that the powers (indices) of 10 in the right-hand column count down through the integers. Notice also that to find the index you have only to count the number of places the digits of the number must move across the decimal point before the 1 is directly to the left of the decimal point, provided you are careful to give the index the correct sign.

(b) The table shows that 10^{-3} means $1 \div 10^3$, 10^{-5} means $1 \div 10^5$ and so on.

Take any two numbers from the right-hand column and multiply them together, giving your answer in index form. For example:

$$10^3 \times 10^{-1} = 10 \times 10 \times 10 \times \frac{1}{10} = 10^2.$$

Try this with several other pairs of numbers. What do you notice about the original indices and the final index of the answer?

(c) If we multiply $10^x \times 10^y$ where x and y are integers then we add the indices to obtain the answer 10^{x+y}.

(d) Take any two numbers from the right-hand column and divide one by the other. For example:

68

$$10^5 \div 10^{-2} = 10^5 \div \frac{1}{10^2} = 10^5 \times 10^2 = 10^7.$$

Try this with several other pairs of numbers. What do you notice about the original indices and the final index of the answer?

(e) If we divide 10^x by 10^y where x and y are integers then we subtract the indices to obtain the final answer 10^{x-y}.

Would the results of (c) and (e) be true if we were using powers of numbers other than 10? Try some examples of your own.

(f) Write these numbers in index form:

    (i) 100 000 000 000 000 000 000 000 000 000 000 000 000;
    (ii) 0·000 000 000 000 000 000 000 000 000 000 000 001.

We use indices mainly because they are a labour-saving device, as you can tell from the above!

Exercise E

1   Write each of the following in index form:

    (i) 1 000 000 000;
    (ii) $2 \times 2 \times 2 \times 2 \times 2 \times 2 \times 2 \times 2$;
    (iii) $1/(4 \times 4 \times 4 \times 4 \times 4 \times 4)$;
    (iv) 0·100 000 000;
    (v) $0·6 \times 0·6 \times 0·6 \times 0·6 \times 0·6$.

2   Simplify:

    (i) $10^5 \times 10^7 \times 10^8$;   (ii) $10^9 \times 10^{-5}$;   (iii) $10^{-7} \times 10^{-6}$;
    (iv) $10^3 \div 10^7$;   (v) $2^4 \div 2^5$;   (vi) $7^{-9} \div 7^7$;
    (vii) $\dfrac{1}{10^{-9}}$;   (viii) $(10^{-4})^{-5}$.

6 Standard index form

(a) Write down the larger of each of the following pairs of numbers:

    (i) $\frac{3}{7}$ and 0·428 65;   (ii) 13_7 and 15_6;
    (iii) $\sqrt{2}$ and 1·40;   (iv) 4^4 and 2^7.

(b) To answer (a) you probably had to convert each pair of numbers to the same form. For example, $\frac{3}{7}$ is $0·\dot{4}28\,57\dot{1}$ as a decimal, and in this form it is much easier to compare it with 0·428 65. Scientists often write numbers using a method called *Standard Index Form* both as a labour-saving device and because it is reasonably easy to compare numbers when written this way.

When a number is written in Standard Index Form it is expressed as a number between 1 and 10 (but not equal to 10) multiplied by a power of 10.

Computation

For example, 490 000 is written in Standard Index Form as

$$4 \cdot 9 \times 10^5.$$

However, $0 \cdot 49 \times 10^6$, although it is also equal to 490 000, is not in Standard Index Form because $0 \cdot 49$ does not lie between 1 and 10.

(c) The distance of the star Sirius from the earth is approximately

82 000 000 000 000 km.

Each of the following represents the same distance. Which one is in Standard Index Form:

(i) 82×10^{12};   (ii) $0 \cdot 82 \times 10^{14}$;   (iii) $8 \cdot 2 \times 10^{13}$?

How would you represent (i) 1; (ii) 10 in Standard Index Form?

Example 5

Find approximate answers to: (i) $386 \times 0 \cdot 709$; (ii) $0 \cdot 627 \div 32 \cdot 7$.

(i) $386 \times 0 \cdot 709 = 3 \cdot 86 \times 10^2 \times 7 \cdot 09 \times 10^{-1}$.

Since $10^2 \times 10^{-1} = 10^1$, the approximate answer is $4 \times 7 \times 10 = 280$.

(ii) $0 \cdot 627 \div 32 \cdot 7 = \dfrac{6 \cdot 27 \times 10^{-1}}{3 \cdot 27 \times 10^1}$.

Since $\dfrac{10^{-1}}{10} = 10^{-2}$, the approximate answer is $\frac{6}{3} \times 10^{-2} = 2 \times 10^{-2} = 0 \cdot 02$.

Example 6

The earth is 156 million km from the sun. How long does it take light from the sun to reach earth if light travels at $3 \cdot 0 \times 10^5$ km/s.

Copy and complete: Time taken $= \dfrac{1 \cdot 56 \times}{3 \cdot 0 \times 10^5}$ s

$= 0 \cdot 52 \times$

$= 520 \, \text{s}.$

Exercise F

1   The approximate mean distances of the planets from the sun are given in the following table:

Planet	Mean distance from the sun
Earth	150×10^6 km
Jupiter	776×10^6 km

Mars	228 million km
Mercury	58 000 000 km
Neptune	45×10^8 km
Pluto	0.6016×10^{10} km
Saturn	142×10^7 km
Uranus	2786 million km
Venus	108 million km

Convert each to Standard Index Form, and hence write the planets down in order of their distances from the sun, the nearest first.

About how many times farther out from the sun is Uranus than (a) Earth; (b) Mercury?

2 The mean distance between two atoms is 1·55 Å where 100 000 000 Å $= 1$ cm. Express the distance 1·55 Å in cm in Standard Index Form.

How many of these atoms would you expect to find in a 5 cm cubic box?

3 Work out the following to 3 s.f. by converting the numbers to Standard Index Form:

(i) 2143×361; (ii) 0.0057×3.6;

(iii) $0.0046 \div 0.000\ 022$; (iv) $(461)^2$;

(v) $\dfrac{316 \times 0.004}{0.35}$.

Give answers to Questions 4 to 7 in Standard Index Form.

4 The needle of a record player moves 8·9 cm when playing a particular L.P. record. If the record makes 830 revolutions estimate to 2 s.f. the width of the groove.

5 Grass seed is sown at the rate of 7 seeds per cm² to make a lawn of area 17 m². Estimate the number of seeds on the lawn.

6 I can draw a line of thickness 0·02 cm with my pen. Approximately how many lines could I draw on this page from side to side if I left a gap of 0·01 cm between each?

7 Calculate each of the following to 3 s.f.

(i) $\dfrac{2.76 \times 10^3}{4.6 \times 10^7}$; (ii) $\dfrac{6.7 \times 10^{-4}}{0.027}$; (iii) $\dfrac{0.416 \times 10^{13}}{0.000\ 006}$.

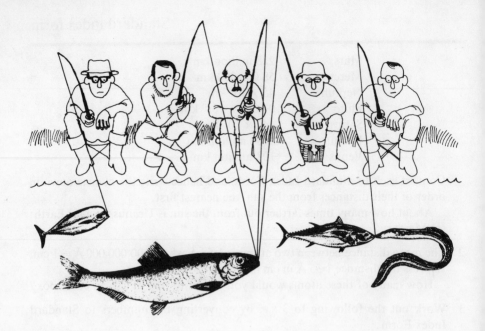

6 Functions

1 A reminder – arrow diagrams, relations and inverses

(*a*) Study the four diagrams in Figure 1. Arrow diagram 1(*a*) represents the relation

$$x \to 2x, \text{ for } x \text{ any member of the set } \{^-2, ^-1, 0, 1, 2\}.$$

What relations do the other diagrams represent?

(*b*) Figure 1(*b*) represents the relation

$$x \to x^2, \text{ for } x \text{ any member of the set } \{^-2, ^-1, 0, 1, 2\}.$$

Notice that only one arrow leaves each member of the object set, but more than one arrow meets some members of the image set. For example, both 2 and $^-2$ are mapped onto 4. Another way of saying this is that in some cases many members of the object set are mapped onto the same member of the image set.

The relation is said to have a 'many to one' correspondence and we can talk generally about the relation being 'many to one'.

Which of the relations in Figure 1 are

    (i) one to one,   (ii) one to many,   (iii) many to many?

72

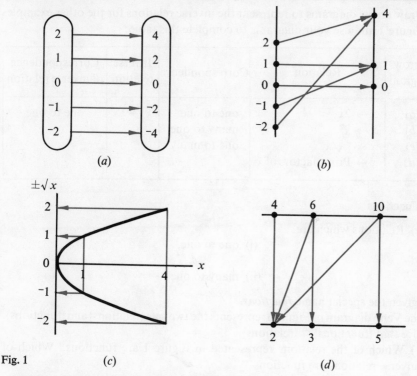

Fig. 1   (a)   (b)   (c)   (d)

(c) Figure 1(c) shows the graph of the relation

$$x \to {}^{\pm}\!\sqrt{x}, \text{ for } 0 \leqslant x \leqslant 4.$$

The arrows show that the images of 4 are 2 and ⁻2, and the images of 1 are 1 and ⁻1. This is an example of a one to many relation. Explain in words what is meant by a one to many relation. Can you think of another relation which has a one to many correspondence?

(d) If the directions of the arrows in Figure 1(a) are reversed, the new diagram represents the *inverse* relation of $x \to 2x$ which is shown in Figure 2. The inverse relation is

$$x \to \tfrac{1}{2}x.$$

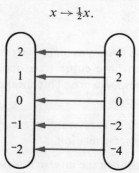

Fig. 2

73

Draw arrow diagrams to represent the inverse relations for the other examples in Figure 1 and use your diagrams to complete this table:

Arrow diagram	Relation	Correspondence	Inverse relation	Correspondence of inverse relation
(a)	$x \rightarrow 2x$	one to one	$x \rightarrow \frac{1}{2}x$	one to one
(b)	$x \rightarrow x^2$	many to one		
(c)	$x \rightarrow {}^{\pm}\sqrt{x}$	one to many		
(d)	$x \rightarrow$ Prime factors of x			

2 Functions

(a) Relations which are

(i) one to one,

or

(ii) many to one

are given the special name *functions*.

The Venn diagram in Figure 3 represents the two sets {relations} and {functions}. Notice that {functions} ⊂ {relations}.

(b) Which of the relations represented in Figure 1 are functions? Which of the inverse relations are functions?

If a relation is a function, is the inverse relation necessarily a function?

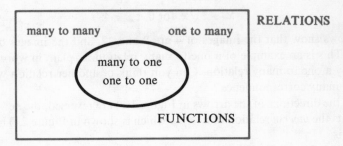

Fig. 3

Summary

1 Functions (which are also known as mappings) are special kinds of relations. They are relations which have either (i) a one to one correspondence or (ii) a many to one correspondence. This means that each member of the object set has a *unique* image.

2 If the direction of the arrows is reversed on an arrow diagram then the new diagram represents the inverse relation.

3 If a function is one to one then the inverse function is also one to one.

74

4   If a function is many to one then the inverse relation is not a function since it has a one to many correspondence.

Exercise A

1   The relation $x \to 2x - 1$ is defined on the set $\{0, 1, 2, 3, 4\}$. Draw an arrow diagram to represent the relation. Is the relation a function? Draw an arrow diagram to represent the inverse relation. Is the inverse relation a function?

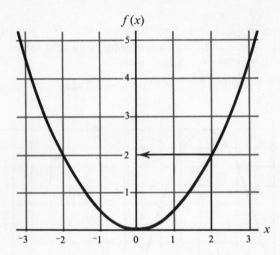

Fig. 4

2   The graph in Figure 4 represents the function $x \to \frac{1}{2}x^2$ for $^-3 \leqslant x \leqslant 3$. The arrow shows that the image of 2 is 2. Use the graph to find the images of (i) 1; (ii) 3; (iii) $^-3$; (iv) 0. Use the graph also to find the images of (i) 2; (ii) $\frac{1}{2}$; (iii) $4\frac{1}{2}$ under the inverse relation. Is there more than one answer in each case?

3   Draw an arrow diagram to represent the relation 'is greater than' for an object set $\{2, 3, 4\}$ and an image set $\{1, 2, 3\}$. Is the relation a function? Describe the inverse relation. Is this a function?

4   (a) Bill throws three darts A, B and C. He scores 3, 1 and 13 respectively. Draw an arrow diagram to represent the relation

dart thrown $\to$ number scored by dart.

Is the relation a function?
   (b) Suppose Bill had scored 20, 20 and 5. Is the relation a function now? Is the relation a function no matter what Bill scores?
   (c) If Bill throws the *same* dart three times is the relation a function?
   (d) Answer (a), (b) and (c) for the relation

rth throw $\to$ number scored in rth throw.

5 If a relation is not a function, but the inverse relation is a function, what can you say about the relation?

6 Discuss whether or not the following relations are functions for various image sets:

     (i) people in your class $\rightarrow$ their ages in years;
     (ii) children in a family $\rightarrow$ parents in the family;
     (iii) $x \rightarrow$ the least integer greater than x;
     (iv) $x \rightarrow {}^+\sqrt{x}$.

7 Use the graph in Figure 5 to find the values of $\sin x°$ if x is (i) 20°; (ii) 110°; (iii) 220°; (iv) 330°. Check your answers by using your tables.
    Is the relation $x° \rightarrow \sin x°$ a function?
    Is the inverse relation a function?

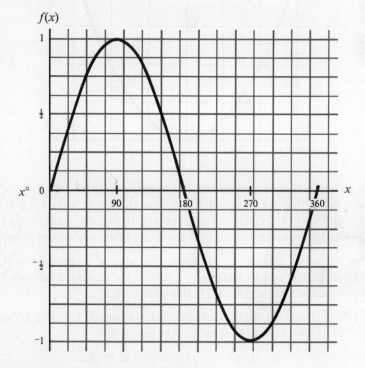

Fig. 5

8 Draw a graph to represent the relation

$$x° \rightarrow \cos x° \text{ for } 0° \leqslant x° \leqslant 360°.$$

From your graph find the values of $\cos x°$ if x is (i) 20°; (ii) 110°; (iii) 220°; (iv) 330°.
    Is the relation $x° \rightarrow \cos x°$ a function?
    Is the inverse relation a function?

3 Domain and range

(a) Figure 6 represents the function

$$x \rightarrow 2x + 1$$

for x, any member of the set $\{^-3, ^-2, ^-1, 0, 1, 2, 3\}$. Copy the diagram and fill in the missing members of the image set.

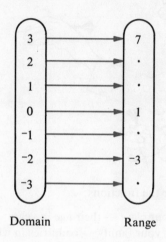

Fig. 6

(b) You should have found that the object set $\{^-3, ^-2, ^-1, 0, 1, 2, 3\}$ is mapped onto the image set $\{^-5, ^-3, ^-1, 1, 3, 5, 7\}$ by the function $x \rightarrow 2x + 1$.

The object set is given the special name DOMAIN and the image set the special name RANGE.

If the domain of the function was extended to include $^-4$ and 4, what would be the range?

If the domain was {integers} what would be the range?

If the domain was {even numbers} what would be the range?

Exercise B

1 Find the range of the functions (a) $x \rightarrow x$; (b) $x \rightarrow x^2$ for the domains:

    (i) $\{0, 1\}$;

    (ii) $\{^-1, 0, 2, 3\}$;

    (iii) $\{x: ^-2 \leqslant x \leqslant 2\}$;

    (iv) {integers};

    (v) {counting numbers};

    (vi) {real numbers};

    (vii) $\{x: ^-10 \leqslant x < 20\}$.

2 Bill throws three darts at a dartboard. If the domain is {darts Bill throws} what can you say about the range of the function

darts Bill throws → number scored by each dart?

3 What is the range for the functions:

(i) people in your class → their age in years;
(ii) members of your family → countries in which they were born;
(iii) $x \to 2x$, x an integer?

4 (a) If the range of each of the following functions is $\{^-4, ^-3, ^-2, ^-1, 0, 1, 2, 3, 4\}$ what is the domain of each?

(i) $x \to \frac{1}{2}x$;
(ii) $x \to 2x - 1$;
(iii) $x \to \dfrac{x}{3}$;
(iv) $x \to \dfrac{12}{x}$.

(b) Answer the same question for the domain $0 < x \leqslant 4$.

4 Function notation

(a) The function 'multiply by two' can be written in the form $x \to 2x$. Write each of the following functions in the form $x \to \ldots$: (i) 'add 1'; (ii) 'subtract 3'; (iii) 'divide by 4'; (iv) 'square'.

(b) In Chapter 2 we used letters like **X**, **H** and **R** to represent transformations. To represent functions we use small letters like f, g and h. For example, we write

$f: x \to 2x$ to mean 'f is the function which maps x onto $2x$'.

Let g be the function 'add 1'. Write this in the form $g: x \to \ldots$.

(c) Copy and complete this table:

Abbreviation	Function	Shorthand notation
f	'multiply by 2'	$f: x \rightarrow 2x$
g	'add 1'	
h		$h: x \rightarrow \dfrac{x}{4}$
m	'identity'	$m: x \rightarrow x$
p		$p: x \rightarrow x^2$

You will remember that we write $\mathbf{X}(T)$ to mean the image of T under the transformation $\mathbf{X}$. In the same way the image of x under the function f is written as $f(x)$. Look at Figure 7.

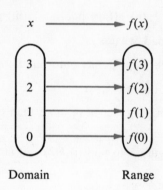

Fig. 7

Since

$$f: x \rightarrow 2x$$

then

$$f: 3 \rightarrow 6$$

i.e. $f(3) = 6$. What are (i) $f(0)$; (ii) $f(1)$; (iii) $f(2)$?

In general, we can write $f(x) = 2x$. Write similar equations for $g(x)$, $h(x)$, $m(x)$ and $p(x)$.

(d) If $p(x) = 9$ then x is 3 or $^-3$ because $3^2 = 9$ and $(^-3)^2 = 9$. Find x if (i) $p(x) = 16$; (ii) $p(x) = \frac{1}{4}$.

Summary

1 $f: x \rightarrow ax + b$ means 'the function f maps x onto $ax + b$'.

2 $f(x)$ is the image of x under the function f. We read $f(x)$ as 'f of x'.

Functions

Exercise C

1   If $t: x \to 3x + 6$, find (i) $t(0)$; (ii) $t(9)$; (iii) $t(^-4)$; (iv) $t(\frac{1}{2})$.

2   For $f: x \to 2(x - 1)$, find (i) $f(2)$; (ii) $f(^-2)$; (iii) $f(a)$.

3   Given that $g(x) = 2 - x^2$ find (i) $g(8)$; (ii) $g(^-8)$; (iii) $g(b)$.

4   Find the images of (i) 0; (ii) 5; (iii) $\frac{1}{2}$ under the function $x \to x^2 + x$.

5   If $k : x \to \frac{1}{2}x^2$, find (i) $k(2)$; (ii) $k(^-2)$; (iii) $k(\frac{1}{2})$.
    If $k(x) = 8$, find x (there are two values).

6   If $h(x) = 5x - 4$, find x when $h(x)$ is (i) 6; (ii) $^-4$; (iii) $^-14$.

7   If f: members of your class $\to$ age in years, find f (yourself).

8   h: capital cities $\to$ countries. Find (i) h(London); (ii) h(Oslo).

9   If g: football teams $\to$ home grounds, what is

     (i) g(Arsenal);   (ii) g(Liverpool);   (iii) g(Sunderland)?

    If $g(x) =$ Elland Road, what is x?

10   m is a function which maps points onto points: $m: (x, y) \to (x, ^-y)$. Find

     (i) $m((1, 2))$;   (ii) $m((^-3, 4))$.

11   If p is a function can $p(x)$ ever have more than one value? Explain your answer.

12   Use the graph in Figure 8 to find (i) $h(2)$; (ii) $h(^-2)$; (iii) $h(3)$; (iv) $h(^-3)$; (v) $h(0)$.
    Write h in the form $h: x \to \ldots$.

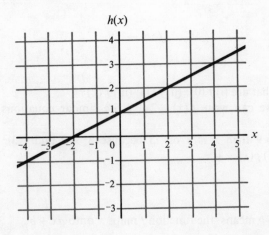

Fig. 8

13 If $f(x) = 4$ for all values of x, draw a graph to show the points $(x, f(x))$ for $^-4 < x < 4$.

Is the inverse relation a function?

14 (a) $f: x \to \sin x$. Find (i) $f(10°)$; (ii) $f(80°)$; (iii) $f(90°)$.

(b) $g: x \to \cos 2x$. Find (i) $g(10°)$; (ii) $g(45°)$; (iii) $g(85°)$.

(c) $f: x \to \sin x$ and $h: x \to \cos x$ for $0° \leqslant x \leqslant 90°$ in each case. Find a value of x so that $f(x) = h(x)$.

5 Composite functions

(a) Let f be the 'multiply by 2' function, and g be the 'add 1' function. Then

$$f: x \to 2x$$

and

$$g: x \to x + 1.$$

Find $f(4)$.

Can you give a meaning to $g(f(4))$?

(b) Look at Figure 9. $g(f(4))$ is the image of $f(4)$ under the function g.

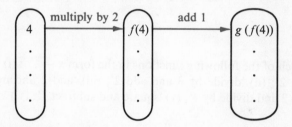

Fig. 9

Since $f(4) = 8$, $g(f(4)) = g(8) = 9$.

Notice that $g(f(x))$ is the image of x after *first* applying function f and *then* applying function g.

We can write $g(f(x))$ more simply as $gf(x)$.

Find (i) $gf(5)$; (ii) $gf(^-3)$; (iii) $gf(0)$.

(c) Study the two flow diagrams in Figure 10. They are in a different form from the ones in previous books as here the function is written along the line instead of in the box. We will use this notation throughout the chapter.

$$x \xrightarrow{\text{multiply by 2}} 2x \xrightarrow{\text{add 1}} 2x+1$$

Fig. 10 $\qquad x \xrightarrow{\ f\ } f(x) \xrightarrow{\ g\ } gf(x)$

We can see that

$$gf(x) = 2x + 1,$$

i.e. gf is the 'multiply by 2 and add 1' function.

Functions

Draw two similar flow diagrams to help you express $fg(x)$ in the same way. Is $fg(x) = gf(x)$ for all values of x? Is fg the same function as gf?

(d) You should have found that $fg(x) = 2(x + 1)$, that is fg is the 'add 1 and multiply by 2' function. fg and gf are called *composite* functions because they are composed of two functions.

(e) Let $f: x \to x + 7$ and $g: x \to x - 3$. Find (i) $fg(0)$; (ii) $fg(2)$; (iii) $fg(^-2)$; (iv) $gf(0)$; (v) $gf(2)$; (vi) $gf(^-2)$.

What do you notice?

Is $fg(x) = gf(x)$ for all values of x? Draw a flow diagram to help you with your answer.

Summary

1   If a function f is followed by a function g, we obtain the composite function gf.

2   Sometimes fg and gf will be the same function. For example, if $f: x \to x + 7$ and $g: x \to x - 3$ then $gf(x) = fg(x) = x + 4$ (see (e) above).

Exercise D

1   Write each of the following functions in the form $x \to \dots$: (i) 'multiply by 3 and add 2'; (ii) 'divide by 3 and add 2'; (iii) 'add 2 and multiply by 3'; (iv) 'add 2 and divide by 3'; (v) 'square and subtract 7'; (vi) 'subtract 7 and square'.

2   Is the function 'square and double' the same as the function 'double and square'? Distinguish between $3x^2$ and $(3x)^2$ by referring to functions.

3   $s: x \to x^2$, $d: x \to x + 2$. Draw flow diagrams to help you to find expressions for $ds(x)$ and $sd(x)$.

4   For $f: x \to 4x + 1$ and $g: x \to 2x - 1$ find: (i) $fg(0)$; (ii) $fg(^-2)$; (iii) $gf(0)$; (iv) $gf(^-2)$.
    Express both fg and gf in the form $x \to \dots$.

5   For $f: x \to 2x - 1$ and $g: x \to 3x - 2$ find: (i) $fg(2)$; (ii) $gf(2)$; (iii) $gf(0)$; (iv) $fg(0)$; (v) $fg(\frac{1}{2})$; (vi) $gf(\frac{1}{2})$.
    Explain your results by expressing fg and gf in the form $x \to \dots$.

6   If $f: x \to \dfrac{1}{x}$ and $g: x \to x + 2$, find expressions for $fg(x)$ and $gf(x)$.

7   $f: x \to x + 1$ and $gf: x \to x$. Express g in the form $x \to \dots$.

8   $f: x \to 2x + 1$ and $fg: x \to x$. Express g in the form $x \to \dots$.

82

9 $h: x \to x$ and $k: x \to 2x + 1$. Find a function m so that hm is the same function as k.

   Is mh the same function as k?

10 $h: x \to x$. Find two different functions g and f for which $h(x) = gf(x) = fg(x)$ for all values of x.

11 $p: (x, y) \to (x, {}^-y)$ and $j: (x, y) \to ({}^-x, y)$. Find: (i) $pj(0,4)$; (ii) $pj(2,3)$; (iii) $jp(2,3)$; (iv) $jp(0,4)$. Express pj and jp in the form $(x, y) \to \ldots$.

12 $f: x \to \sin x$, $g: x \to 2x$. Express (i) fg; (ii) gf in the form $x \to \ldots$.

6 More about inverse functions

(a) We have already seen that a function only has an inverse, which is itself a function, if it is a one to one relation. If a function is many to one then the inverse is a one to many relation.

We write the inverse of a function f in shorthand notation as f^{-1}.

(b) Figure 11(a) represents the 'add three' function

$$f: x \to x + 3,$$

and Figure 11(b) the inverse function f^{-1}. Write f^{-1} in words and in the form $x \to \ldots$.

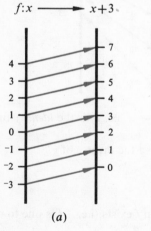
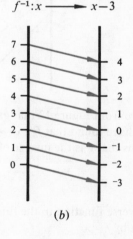

Fig. 11   (a)   (b)

We can see that $f(4) = 7$ and $f^{-1}(7) = 4$.

What are (i) $f^{-1}(3)$; (ii) $f^{-1}({}^-1)$; (iii) $f^{-1}({}^-3)$; (iv) $ff^{-1}(4)$; (v) $f^{-1}f(4)$; (vi) $ff^{-1}(1)$; (vii) $f^{-1}f(1)$?

Check that $ff^{-1}(x) = f^{-1}f(x)$ for some more values of x.

Is ff^{-1} the same function as $f^{-1}f$?

(c) Draw an arrow diagram to represent the function

$$f: x \to 2x - 1, \text{ for the domain } \{{}^-3, {}^-2, {}^-1, 0, 1, 2, 3\}.$$

Functions

If the range of f becomes the domain of g and

$$g: x \rightarrow \tfrac{1}{2}(x+1),$$

draw an arrow diagram to represent g.

What do you notice about the domain of f and the range of g?

If the domain of f was {integers}, what would be the range of g?

Can you make a general statement about the domain of f and the range of g?

Write the composite function gf in the form $gf: x \rightarrow \dots$.

(d) Follow the method in (c) this time using $\{^-3, ^-2, ^-1, 0, 1, 2, 3\}$ as the domain of g to help you express fg in the form $fg: x \rightarrow \dots$.

(e) If you combine your two arrow diagrams for (c) above you can form Figure 12:

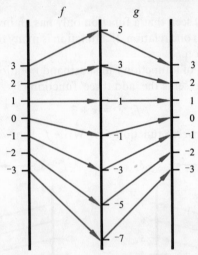

Fig. 12

We can see from Figure 12 that $gf: x \rightarrow x$, i.e. gf is the *identity* function. You should also have found that $fg: x \rightarrow x$.

This means that g is the inverse of f. Is f the inverse of g?

Summary

1 If the inverse function to the function f exists (i.e. if f is one to one) then we denote it by f^{-1}.

2 When two functions combine to form the identity function, $x \rightarrow x$, each is the inverse of the other.

Exercise E

1 What are the inverse functions of: (i) 'divide by 4'; (ii) 'add 6'; (iii) 'multiply by 7'; (iv) $x \rightarrow x+9$; (v) $x \rightarrow x-2$; (vi) $x \rightarrow 2x-1$?

2 Does the relation represented in Figure 13 define a function f? If so, does it possess an inverse f^{-1}? If appropriate write down: (i) $f(4)$; (ii) $f^{-1}(9)$; (iii) $ff^{-1}(^-1)$; (iv) $f^{-1}f(^-1)$.

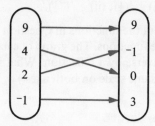

Fig. 13

3 By drawing combined arrow diagrams like Figure 12 find which of the following pairs of functions are inverses of each other:

(i) $x \to 2x - 4, x \to 4 - 2x$; (ii) $x \to 4/x, x \to x/4$;
(iii) $x \to 4 + 1/x, x \to x - 1/4$; (iv) $x \to 12/x, x \to 12/x$.

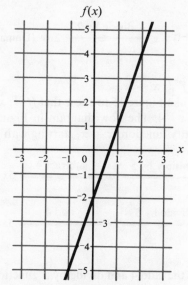

Fig. 14

4 The graph in Figure 14 represents the function $f: x \to 3x - 2$. Use the graph to find: (i) $f(2)$; (ii) $f(0)$; (iii) $f^{-1}(4)$; (iv) $f^{-1}(^-2)$. By finding some more number pairs $(x, f^{-1}(x))$, draw the graph of f^{-1}.

5 (a) From the graph in Figure 5 find the values of x for which $\sin x°$ is (i) $\frac{1}{2}$; (ii) $^-\frac{1}{2}$; (iii) 0; (iv) 0·4.
(b) Is the relation $\sin x° \to x°$ a function?
(c) Does the function $x° \to \sin x°$ have an inverse function?
(d) If the domain of the function $x° \to \sin x°$ is restricted to $0° \leqslant x° \leqslant 90°$, does the function $x° \to \sin x°$ have an inverse which is also a function?

6 (a) Draw the graph of the function $g: x° \to \cos x°$ for the domain $0° \leqslant x° \leqslant 180°$.

(b) What is the range of g in this case?

(c) If g^{-1} exists, find (i) $g^{-1}(\frac{1}{2})$; (ii) $g^{-1}(-\frac{1}{2})$.

7 Draw graphs to represent the functions in Question 1. On the same axes draw the graphs of the inverse functions. The graph of each function can be mapped onto the graph of its inverse by a reflection. What is the equation of the line of reflection? (Use the same scale on both axes.)

7 Finding inverse functions

(a) Suppose f is the function 'multiply by 2'. The flow diagram in Figure 15 shows the steps needed to form the identity function, $x \to x$, starting with f:

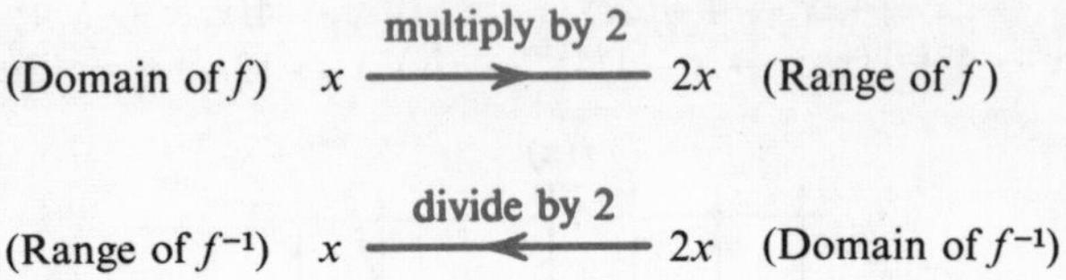

$$\text{(Domain of } f) \quad x \xrightarrow{\text{multiply by 2}} 2x \quad \text{(Range of } f)$$

$$\text{(Range of } f^{-1}) \quad x \xleftarrow{\text{divide by 2}} 2x \quad \text{(Domain of } f^{-1})$$

Fig. 15

Write f^{-1} in the form $f^{-1}: x \to \ldots$.

Draw a flow diagram like Figure 15 to show that $ff^{-1}: x \to x$.

(b) Suppose $g: x \to 5x - 4$. The flow diagram in Figure 16 shows the steps needed to form the identity function, $x \to x$, starting with g:

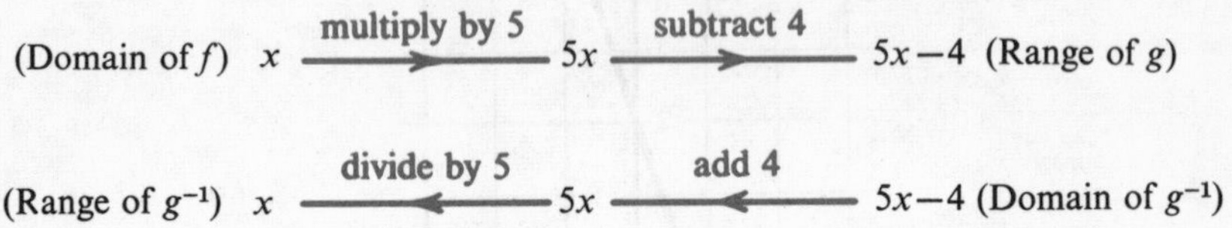

$$\text{(Domain of } f) \quad x \xrightarrow{\text{multiply by 5}} 5x \xrightarrow{\text{subtract 4}} 5x - 4 \quad \text{(Range of } g)$$

$$\text{(Range of } g^{-1}) \quad x \xleftarrow{\text{divide by 5}} 5x \xleftarrow{\text{add 4}} 5x - 4 \quad \text{(Domain of } g^{-1})$$

Fig. 16

We can see that g^{-1} is the 'add 4 and divide by 5' function. To find the inverse of a composite function we must therefore find the inverses of the functions of which it is composed and then combine them in the reverse order. We can write this as $(fg)^{-1} = g^{-1}f^{-1}$.

Now write in words the inverse of the function 'add 3 and divide by 2'.

(c) If we wish to express g^{-1} in the form $g^{-1}: x \to \ldots$, we must apply the function 'add 4 and divide by 5' to x. Remember that x is now a member of the domain of g^{-1}. The process is shown in Figure 17.

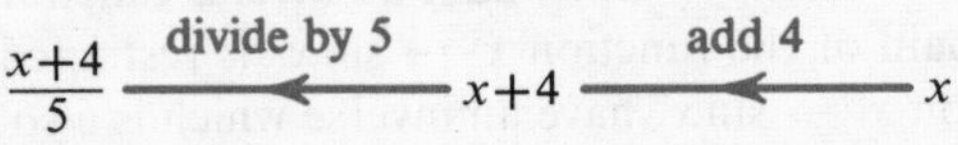

$$\frac{x+4}{5} \xleftarrow{\text{divide by 5}} x+4 \xleftarrow{\text{add 4}} x$$

Fig. 17

Hence

$$g^{-1}: x \to \frac{(x+4)}{5}.$$

(*d*) We can use the method shown in (*c*) above to enable us to solve equations. Study the flow diagrams shown in Figure 18.

(i) $x \xrightarrow{\text{multiply by 5}} 5x \xrightarrow{\text{subtract 3}} 5x-3$

(ii) $x \xleftarrow{\text{divide by 5}} 5x \xleftarrow{\text{add 3}} 5x-3$

Fig. 18   (iii) $2 \xleftarrow{\text{divide by 5}} 10 \xleftarrow{\text{add 3}} 7$

Use Figure 18 to help you explain why the solution of the equation $5x - 3 = 7$ is $x = 2$.

Use the same method to solve the equation

$$\frac{x}{2} + 3 = 5.$$

Example 1

Find the inverse of the function $f: x \to \frac{1}{2}(x-3)^2$. Is the inverse relation a function?

(i) To form f:

$x \xrightarrow{\text{subtract 3}} x-3 \xrightarrow{\text{square}} (x-3)^2 \xrightarrow{\text{divide by 2}} \frac{1}{2}(x-3)^2$

(ii) To form f^{-1}:

$\pm\sqrt{2x}+3 \xleftarrow{\text{add 3}} \pm\sqrt{2x} \xleftarrow{\text{square root}} 2x \xleftarrow{\text{multiply by 2}} x$

Hence $f^{-1}: x \to \pm\sqrt{2x} + 3$. f^{-1} is not a function because it has a one to many correspondence. For example,

$$f^{-1}(2) = \pm\sqrt{4} + 3$$
$$= 5 \text{ or } 1.$$

Example 2

Solve the equation $\frac{x}{3} - 6 = 1$. To form the function $x \to \frac{x}{3} - 6$:

$x \xrightarrow{\text{divide by 3}} \frac{x}{3} \xrightarrow{\text{subtract 6}} \frac{x}{3} - 6$

87

Functions

To form the inverse function:

$$3(x+6) \xleftarrow{\text{multiply by 3}} x+6 \xleftarrow{\text{add 6}} x$$

Applying this inverse function to the image 1:

$$21 \xleftarrow{\text{multiply by 3}} 7 \xleftarrow{\text{add 6}} 1$$

Hence $x = 21$.

Exercise F

1 Find, by using flow diagrams, the inverses of:

    (i) $x \to 3x + 1$;   (ii) $x \to 3(x + 1)$;   (iii) $x \to \frac{1}{2}x - 4$;

    (iv) $x \to \frac{x^2}{4}$;   (v) $x \to 2x^3$;   (vi) $x \to \frac{x}{12} + 7$;

    (vii) $x \to \frac{1}{2}x^2 - 2$.

Which of the inverse relations are functions?

2 Find the inverse of $x \to 1 - \dfrac{1}{(1 - x)}$.

3 If $m: x \to 2x$ and $p: x \to x + 5$ express mp in the form $mp: x \to \dots$. Find m^{-1} and p^{-1} in the same form.

    Draw a flow diagram to find $(mp)^{-1}$ in the form $(mp)^{-1}: x \to \dots$.

    Compare your flow diagram with that in Figure 19. What functions are missing from above the arrows?

    Express $(mp)^{-1}$ in terms of m^{-1} and p^{-1}.

    Express $(pm)^{-1}$ in terms of m^{-1} and p^{-1}.

$$x \xrightarrow{\quad p \quad} p(x) \xrightarrow{\quad m \quad} mp(x)$$

$$(mp)^{-1}(x) \xleftarrow{\qquad} m^{-1}(x) \xleftarrow{\qquad} x$$

Fig. 19

4 Draw flow diagrams to help you show that the functions 'subtract 1 and divide by 2' and 'divide by 2 and subtract $\frac{1}{2}$' can both be expressed in the same form. Express the inverse of each in the form $x \to \dots$.

5 Draw a graph to represent the function $g: x \to 3x + 4$. Find the inverse of this function and draw its graph on the same axes. The graph of g^{-1} is the image of the graph of g under a certain reflection. What is the equation of the line of reflection? What function has the line of reflection as its graph?

88

6 Solve the equations:

(i) $x - 4 = 7$; (ii) $\dfrac{x}{3} + 4 = 6$; (iii) $\dfrac{x - 4}{7} = 4$.

Summary

If mp is a composite function, then its inverse $(mp)^{-1}$ can be expressed in terms of m^{-1} and p^{-1} as $p^{-1}m^{-1}$. That is $(mp)^{-1}(x) = p^{-1}m^{-1}(x)$.

8 Self-inverse functions

(a) Figure 20 shows a graph of the function

$$f: x \rightarrow 7 - x, \text{ for the domain } \{x: 0 \leqslant x \leqslant 7\}.$$

Notice that the points on the graph are those with coordinates $(x, f(x))$.

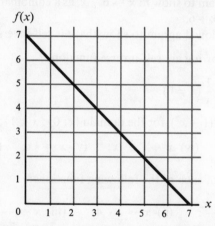

Fig. 20

Use the graph to find (i) $f(3)$; (ii) $f(4)$. What do you notice?
We can also see that $f(1) = 6$ and $f(6) = 1$.
If $f(a) = b$, what can you say about $f(b)$?
What is $ff(a)$?

(b) What are (i) $ff(3)$; (ii) $ff(4)$? Now find $ff(x)$ for some more values of x. You should have found that for all values of x, $ff(x) = x$.

The function $f: x \rightarrow 7 - x$ is its own inverse, and we say that it is a *self-inverse function*.

(c) Draw graphs of the functions (i) $f: x \rightarrow {}^-x$; (ii) $g: x \rightarrow \dfrac{12}{x}$ $(x \neq 0)$; (iii) $h: x \rightarrow x$, for the domain $\{{}^-12 \leqslant x \leqslant 12\}$.

Does each graph have a line of symmetry? If so, what is its equation?
What are (i) $ff({}^-1)$; (ii) $gg(4)$; (iii) $hh(0)$?
What is special about the functions f, g and h?
Are all functions whose graphs have the line $y = x$ as a line of symmetry self-inverse functions?

Functions

Summary

A function f is self-inverse if $ff(x) = x$ for all elements x of its domain. The functions $(a)\ x \rightarrow x$; $(b)\ x \rightarrow {}^-x$; $(c)\ x \rightarrow a - x$; $(d)\ x \rightarrow \dfrac{a}{x}\ (x \neq 0)$ are all self-inverse.

Exercise G

1 Simplify $7 - (7 - x)$. How does this help to explain that the function $f: x \rightarrow 7 - x$ is self-inverse?

2 Simplify $12 \div \left(\dfrac{12}{x}\right)$. How does this help to explain that the function $f: x \rightarrow \dfrac{12}{x}$ is self-inverse?

3 Draw a flow diagram to show $f: x \rightarrow 6 - x$, as a combination of the functions $x \rightarrow {}^-x$ and $x \rightarrow x + 6$.
   Draw another flow diagram to show that f is self-inverse.

4 Which of the following are self-inverse functions?

   (i) $x \rightarrow 1 - \dfrac{1}{x}\ (x \neq 0)$;

   (ii) $x \rightarrow {}^+\sqrt{(1 - x^2)}$, for the domain $\{x: 0 \leqslant x \leqslant 1\}$;

   (iii) $x \rightarrow 4$;   (iv) $x \rightarrow 1 - \tfrac{1}{2}x$;   (v) $x \rightarrow \tfrac{1}{2}x$;   (vi) $x \rightarrow \dfrac{-2}{x}\ (x \neq 0)$.

5 Find the inverse of each of the following functions:

   (i) $x \rightarrow \dfrac{6 - x}{2}$;   (ii) $x \rightarrow \dfrac{1}{x} + 4$;   (iii) $x \rightarrow \dfrac{1}{x - 4}$;

   (iv) $x \rightarrow \dfrac{k}{6 - x}$;   (v) $x \rightarrow \dfrac{1}{1 - \dfrac{6}{x}}$.

   For what values of x are (i) the functions; (ii) their inverses undefined?

Using tables

You will need a copy of SMP Elementary Tables

1 Introduction

What have you used as aids to computation? With how many of the following are you familiar:

slide rule, abacus, nomogram, calculating machine, Napier's bones, tables?

This interlude deals with the use of tables of squares, square roots and reciprocals. You have probably already used tables of sines and cosines to help solve problems in trigonometry. The remaining tables in the book, tangents and logarithms, will be discussed later.

2 Squares

Figure 1 is an extract taken from a table of squares:

	0	1	2	3	4	5	6	7	8	9
1·0	1·00	1·02	1·04	1·06	1·08	1·10	1·12	1·14	1·17	1·19
1·1	1·21	1·23	1·25	1·28	1·30	1·32	1·35	1·37	1·39	1·42
1·2	1·44	1·46	1·49	1·51	1·54	1·56	1·59	1·61	1·64	1·66
1·3	1·69	1·72	1·74	1·77	1·80	1·82	1·85	1·88	1·90	1·93
1·4	1·96	1·99	2·02	2·04	2·07	2·10	2·13	2·16	2·19	2·22
1·5	2·25	2·28	2·31	2·34	2·37	2·40	2·43	2·46	2·50	2·53
1·6	2·56	2·59	2·62	2·66	2·69	2·72	2·76	2·79	2·82	2·86
1·7	2·89	2·92	2·96	2·99	3·03	3·06	3·10	3·13	3·17	3·20
1·8	3·24	3·28	3·31	3·35	3·39	3·42	3·46	3·50	3·53	3·57
1·9	3·61	3·65	3·69	3·72	3·76	3·80	3·84	3·88	3·92	3·96
2·0	4·00	4·04	4·08	4·12	4·16	4·20	4·24	4·28	4·33	4·37
2·1	4·41	4·45	4·49	4·54	4·58	4·62	4·67	4·71	4·75	4·80
2·2	4·84	4·88	4·93	4·97	5·02	5·06	5·11	5·15	5·20	5·24
2·3	5·29	5·34	5·38	5·43	5·48	5·52	5·57	5·62	5·66	5·71
2·4	5·76	5·81	5·86	5·90	5·95	6·00	6·05	6·10	6·15	6·20
2·5	6·25	6·30	6·35	6·40	6·45	6·50	6·55	6·60	6·66	6·71
2·6	6·76	6·81	6·86	6·92	6·97	7·02	7·08	7·13	7·18	7·24
2·7	7·29	7·34	7·40	7·45	7·51	7·56	7·62	7·67	7·73	7·78
2·8	7·84	7·90	7·95	8·01	8·07	8·12	8·18	8·24	8·29	8·35
2·9	8·41	8·47	8·53	8·58	8·64	8·70	8·76	8·82	8·88	8·94
3·0	9·00	9·06	9·12	9·18	9·24	9·30	9·36	9·42	9·49	9·55
3·1	9·61	9·67	9·73	9·80	9·86	9·92	9·99	10·0	10·1	10·2
3·2	10·2	10·3	10·4	10·4	10·5	10·6	10·6	10·7	10·8	10·8
3·3	10·9	11·0	11·0	11·1	11·2	11·2	11·3	11·4	11·4	11·5
3·4	11·6	11·6	11·7	11·8	11·8	11·9	12·0	12·0	12·1	12·2

Fig. 1

It shows for example that $2 \cdot 2^2 = 4 \cdot 84$ and that $2 \cdot 7^2 = 7 \cdot 29$.

What is the value of $2 \cdot 5^2$?

Calculate the *exact* value of $3 \cdot 3^2$. Why does your answer differ slightly from that given by the table? Do you agree that the table gives the value of $2 \cdot 24^2$ as $5 \cdot 02$? Should we write $2 \cdot 24^2 = 5 \cdot 02$ or $2 \cdot 24^2 \approx 5 \cdot 02$? Find $2 \cdot 27^2$ and $2 \cdot 72^2$ from the table.

The table from which Figure 1 is taken gives, correct to 3 S.F., the square of any 3-figure number between 1 and 10. For this reason, it is called a '3-figure table'. If a 4-figure table of squares is available, find out how it is used to find the square of a number with 4 S.F.

Suppose we want to know the square of a number which does not lie between 1 and 10. For example, what is $22 \cdot 5^2$? We can estimate the answer first:

$$22 \cdot 5^2 \approx 20^2$$
$$= 400.$$

So $22 \cdot 5^2 \approx 400$. Can we be sure that $22 \cdot 5^2 > 400$?

We see from the table of squares that $2 \cdot 25^2 \approx 5 \cdot 06$, and so it follows that

$$22 \cdot 5^2 \approx 506 \text{ (to 3 S.F.)}.$$

Here are some further examples of this method. You will see that special care is needed in finding the squares of numbers less than 1.

Example 1

Find 281^2. Rough estimate:

$$281^2 \approx 300^2$$
$$= 90\,000.$$

From table:

$$2 \cdot 81^2 \approx 7 \cdot 90$$

so

$$281^2 \approx 79\,000 \text{ (to 3 S.F.)}.$$

Example 2

Find $0 \cdot 0193^2$. Rough estimate:

$$0 \cdot 0193^2 \approx 0 \cdot 02^2$$
$$= 0 \cdot 0004.$$

From table:

$$1 \cdot 93^2 \approx 3 \cdot 72$$

so

$$0 \cdot 0193^2 \approx 0 \cdot 000\,372 \text{ (to 3 S.F.)}.$$

Exercise A

1 Without referring to the table, estimate the following:

    (a) 19^2;   (b) 41^2;   (c) 0.41^2;

    (d) 507^2;   (e) 0.029^2;   (f) 5140^2.

2 Find, correct to 3 s.f.:

    (a) 5.2^2;   (b) 6.9^2;   (c) 4.61^2;   (d) 8.07^2;

    (e) 9.43^2;   (f) 2.49^2;   (g) π^2.

3 Estimate and then use the table to find:

    (a) 52^2;   (b) 0.69^2;   (c) 46.1^2;

    (d) 807^2;   (e) 0.943^2;   (f) 0.249^2.

4 Estimate and then use the table to find:

    (a) 76^2;   (b) 29^2;   (c) 0.55^2;

    (d) 20.5^2;   (e) 0.171^2;   (f) 103^2.

5 Find to 3 s.f., the value of:

    (a) 1400^2;   (b) 0.014^2;   (c) 630^2;   (d) 0.0063^2;

    (e) 8470^2;   (f) $0.000\,783^2$; (g) $654\,000^2$; (h) 0.0303^2.

6 Work out $1.5^2 + 2.8^2$ and give your answer correct to 3 s.f. Calculate, as accurately as your tables allow, the length of the hypotenuse of a right-angled triangle which has other sides of length 1·5 cm and 2·8 cm respectively.

3 Square roots

Figure 2 shows two extracts from 3-figure tables of square roots:

2·3	1·52	1·52	1·52	1·53	1·53	1·53	1·54	1·54	1·54	1·55
2·4	1·55	1·55	1·56	1·56	1·56	1·57	1·57	1·57	1·57	1·58
2·5	1·58	1·58	1·59	1·59	1·59	1·60	1·60	1·60	1·61	1·61
2·6	1·61	1·62	1·62	1·62	1·62	1·63	1·63	1·63	1·64	1·64
2·7	1·64	1·65	1·65	1·65	1·66	1·66	1·66	1·66	1·67	1·67
2·8	1·67	1·68	1·68	1·68	1·69	1·69	1·69	1·69	1·70	1·70
2·9	1·70	1·71	1·71	1·71	1·71	1·72	1·72	1·72	1·73	1·73
3·0	1·73	1·73	1·74	1·74	1·74	1·75	1·75	1·75	1·75	1·76
3·1	1·76	1·76	1·77	1·77	1·77	1·77	1·78	1·78	1·78	1·79
3·2	1·79	1·79	1·79	1·80	1·80	1·80	1·81	1·81	1·81	1·81
3·3	1·82	1·82	1·82	1·82	1·83	1·83	1·83	1·84	1·84	1·84
3·4	1·84	1·85	1·85	1·85	1·85	1·86	1·86	1·86	1·87	1·87
3·5	1·87	1·87	1·88	1·88	1·88	1·88	1·89	1·89	1·89	1·89
3·6	1·90	1·90	1·90	1·91	1·91	1·91	1·91	1·92	1·92	1·92
3·7	1·92	1·93	1·93	1·93	1·93	1·94	1·94	1·94	1·94	1·95
3·8	1·95	1·95	1·95	1·96	1·96	1·96	1·96	1·97	1·97	1·97
3·9	1·97	1·98	1·98	1·98	1·98	1·99	1·99	1·99	1·99	2·00
4·0	2·00	2·00	2·00	2·01	2·01	2·01	2·01	2·02	2·02	2·02

23	4·80	4·81	4·82	4·83	4·84	4·85	4·86	4·87	4·88	4·89
24	4·90	4·91	4·92	4·93	4·94	4·95	4·96	4·97	4·98	4·99
25	5·00	5·01	5·02	5·03	5·04	5·05	5·06	5·07	5·08	5·09
26	5·10	5·11	5·12	5·13	5·14	5·15	5·16	5·17	5·18	5·19
27	5·20	5·21	5·22	5·22	5·23	5·24	5·25	5·26	5·27	5·28
28	5·29	5·30	5·31	5·32	5·33	5·34	5·35	5·36	5·37	5·38
29	5·39	5·39	5·40	5·41	5·42	5·43	5·44	5·45	5·46	5·47
30	5·48	5·49	5·50	5·50	5·51	5·52	5·53	5·54	5·55	5·56
31	5·57	5·58	5·59	5·59	5·60	5·61	5·62	5·63	5·64	5·65
32	5·66	5·67	5·67	5·68	5·69	5·70	5·71	5·72	5·73	5·74
33	5·74	5·75	5·76	5·77	5·78	5·79	5·80	5·81	5·81	5·82
34	5·83	5·84	5·85	5·86	5·87	5·87	5·88	5·89	5·90	5·91
35	5·92	5·92	5·93	5·94	5·95	5·96	5·97	5·97	5·98	5·99
36	6·00	6·01	6·02	6·02	6·03	6·04	6·05	6·06	6·07	6·07
37	6·08	6·09	6·10	6·11	6·12	6·12	6·13	6·14	6·15	6·16
38	6·16	6·17	6·18	6·19	6·20	6·20	6·21	6·22	6·23	6·24
39	6·24	6·25	6·26	6·27	6·28	6·28	6·29	6·30	6·31	6·32
40	6·32	6·33	6·34	6·35	6·36	6·36	6·37	6·38	6·39	6·40

Fig. 2

Do you agree that $\sqrt{3\cdot30} \approx 1\cdot82$ and that $\sqrt{29\cdot4} \approx 5\cdot42$?

What values of $\sqrt{37\cdot3}$ and $\sqrt{3\cdot09}$ are given in the tables?

Notice that only one square root is given for each number.

What are the *two* square roots of 9?

The extracts come from tables which give the positive square roots of numbers between 1 and 100. How can we find the square roots of numbers which are less than 1 or greater than 100?

For example, what is $\sqrt{375}$? Since $375 \approx 400$, it follows that $\sqrt{375} \approx 20$. Is $\sqrt{375}$ greater than 20 or less than 20? Tables give the values:

$$(a)\quad \sqrt{3\cdot75} \approx 1\cdot94 \qquad \text{and} \qquad (b)\quad \sqrt{37\cdot5} \approx 6\cdot12.$$

Our estimate confirms that we should use (a) rather than (b) and that

$$\sqrt{375} \approx 19\cdot4 \text{ (correct to 3 s.f.)}.$$

Figure 3 shows some corresponding pairs of numbers in the mapping $x \rightarrow \sqrt{x}$. The entries in red have been obtained directly from the table.

x	0·003 75	0·0375	0·375	3·75	37·5	375	3750
	↓	↓	↓	↓	↓	↓	↓
$\sqrt{x}$	0·0612	0·194	0·612	1·94	6·12	19·4	61·2

Fig. 3

Look carefully at the patterns of numbers in Figure 3 then copy and complete Figure 4.

x	0·0025	0·025	0·25	2·5	25	250	2500
	↓	↓	↓	↓	↓	↓	↓
$\sqrt{x}$		0·158			5		50

Fig. 4

It is particularly important to get into the habit of checking square roots by making a rough estimate. Did you, for example, find that $\sqrt{250} \approx 15 \cdot 8$? Check that this is a reasonable result by working out 16^2.

Exercise B

1 Find the value of:

(a) $\sqrt{7 \cdot 2}$;   (b) $\sqrt{83}$;   (c) $\sqrt{54 \cdot 7}$;   (d) $\sqrt{4 \cdot 88}$;   (e) $\sqrt{9 \cdot 36}$;
(f) $\sqrt{35 \cdot 9}$;   (g) $\sqrt{40 \cdot 4}$;   (h) $\sqrt{8 \cdot 49}$;   (i) $\sqrt{5 \cdot 86}$;   (j) $\sqrt{11 \cdot 8}$.

2 Copy and complete the following:

(a)

x	0·0043	0·043	0·43	4·3	43	430	4300
$\sqrt{x}$		0·207			6·56		

(b)

x	5·46	54·6	546	5460	54 600	546 000
$\sqrt{x}$			23·4	73·9		

(c)

x	0·000 018 6	0·000 186	0·001 86	0·0186	0·186	1·86
$\sqrt{x}$				0·136		1·36

3 Find the value of:

(a) $\sqrt{130}$;   (b) $\sqrt{200}$;   (c) $\sqrt{1750}$;
(d) $\sqrt{0 \cdot 241}$;   (e) $\sqrt{0 \cdot 06}$;   (f) $\sqrt{0 \cdot 66}$.

4 Use tables to calculate:

(a) $(\sqrt{7} + \sqrt{5})^2$;   (b) $\sqrt{(7^2 + 5^2)}$;   (c) $(\sqrt{53} - \sqrt{28})^2$;
(d) $\sqrt{2\frac{3}{4}}$;   (e) $\sqrt{0 \cdot 001}$.

5 Use Pythagoras' rule to find the missing lengths:

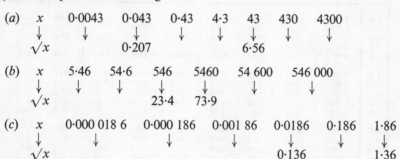

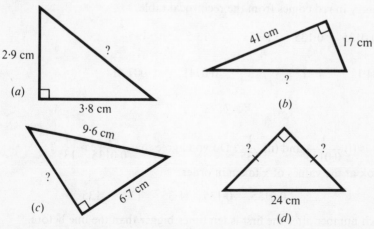

Fig. 5

4 Reciprocals

The mapping $x \to \dfrac{1}{x}$ is called the *reciprocal function* and Figure 6 is an extract from a 3-figure table of reciprocals. It gives values of $\dfrac{1}{x}$ tabulated for values of x between 1 and 10.

	0	1	2	3	4	5	6	7	8	9
1·0	1·00	·990	·980	·971	·962	·952	·943	·935	·926	·917
1·1	0·909	·901	·893	·885	·877	·870	·862	·855	·847	·840
1·2	0·833	·826	·820	·813	·806	·800	·794	·787	·781	·775
1·3	0·769	·763	·758	·752	·746	·741	·735	·730	·725	·719
1·4	0·714	·709	·704	·699	·694	·690	·685	·680	·676	·671
1·5	0·667	·662	·658	·654	·649	·645	·641	·637	·633	·629
1·6	0·625	·621	·617	·613	·610	·606	·602	·599	·595	·592
1·7	0·588	·585	·581	·578	·575	·571	·568	·565	·562	·559
1·8	0·556	·552	·549	·546	·543	·541	·538	·535	·532	·529
1·9	0·526	·524	·521	·518	·515	·513	·510	·508	·505	·503
2·0	0·500	·498	·495	·493	·490	·488	·485	·483	·481	·478
2·1	0·476	·474	·472	·469	·467	·465	·463	·461	·459	·457
2·2	0·455	·452	·450	·448	·446	·444	·442	·441	·439	·437
2·3	0·435	·433	·431	·429	·427	·426	·424	·422	·420	·418
2·4	0·417	·415	·413	·412	·410	·408	·407	·405	·403	·402

Fig. 6

For example, $\dfrac{1}{1·7} \approx 0·588$ and $\dfrac{1}{2·28} \approx 0·439$. What is the value of (i) $\dfrac{1}{2·2}$ and (ii) $\dfrac{1}{1·82}$?

Figure 7 shows some corresponding pairs of numbers in the mapping $x \to \dfrac{1}{x}$. The entry in red comes from the reciprocal table.

x	0·0135	0·135	1·35	13·5	135
↓	↓	↓	↓	↓	↓
$\dfrac{1}{x}$	74·1	7·41	0·741	0·0741	0·007 41

Fig. 7

What is (i) $\dfrac{1}{0·0135}$ and (ii) $\dfrac{1}{135}$? Do you agree that $\dfrac{1}{0·0135} > \dfrac{1}{135}$?

Look at the values of x taken in order:

$$0·0135 \quad 0·135 \quad 1·35 \quad 13·5 \quad 135$$

Each number after the first is ten times bigger than the one before.

Now look at the corresponding values of $\frac{1}{x}$ taken in order:

$$74\cdot1 \qquad 7\cdot41 \qquad 0\cdot741 \qquad 0\cdot0741 \qquad 0\cdot00741$$

Do you agree that each number is one tenth of the number which precedes it? We see that as x *increases* in size, $\frac{1}{x}$ *decreases*. That is,

$$0\cdot0135 < 0\cdot135 < 1\cdot35 < 13\cdot5 < 135$$

and

$$74\cdot1 > 7\cdot41 > 0\cdot741 > 0\cdot0741 > 0\cdot007\,41.$$

What are the approximate values of:

$$1\cdot35 \times 0\cdot741, \ 13\cdot5 \times 0\cdot0741, \ 0\cdot0135 \times 74\cdot1, \text{ etc.}?$$

We can use the fact that a number multiplied by its exact reciprocal gives an answer 1 to confirm our working.

Exercise C

1 Find, correct to 3 s.f.:

(a) $\dfrac{1}{4\cdot9}$; (b) $\dfrac{1}{8\cdot4}$; (c) $\dfrac{1}{2\cdot36}$; (d) $\dfrac{1}{9\cdot53}$;

(e) $\dfrac{1}{4\cdot01}$; (f) $\dfrac{1}{5\cdot67}$; (g) $\dfrac{1}{\pi}$.

2 Copy and complete the following:

(a)

x	0·0817	0·817	8·17	81·7	817
↓	↓	↓	↓	↓	↓
$\frac{1}{x}$			0·122		

(b)

x	0·000 069 8	0·000 698	0·006 98	0·0698	0·698	6·98
↓	↓	↓	↓	↓	↓	↓
$\frac{1}{x}$						0·143

(c)

x	2·34	23·4	234	2340	23 400
↓	↓	↓	↓	↓	↓
$\frac{1}{x}$					

Using tables

3 Find the values of the following and check your answer carefully in each case:

(a) $\dfrac{1}{0\cdot49}$; (b) $\dfrac{1}{23}$; (c) $\dfrac{1}{0\cdot152}$;

(d) $\dfrac{1}{46\cdot2}$; (e) $\dfrac{1}{0\cdot032}$; (f) $\dfrac{1}{407}$.

4 Work out:

(a) $\dfrac{1}{1\cdot7^2}$; (b) $\dfrac{1}{\sqrt{8\cdot4}}$; (c) $\left(\dfrac{1}{2\cdot3}+\dfrac{1}{4\cdot6}\right)^2$;

(d) $\sqrt{\left(\dfrac{1}{1\cdot9}+\dfrac{1}{7\cdot8}\right)}$; (e) $\dfrac{1}{3+\frac{1}{2\cdot7}}$.

5 The quantities R, x and y are related by the formula:

$$\frac{1}{R}=\frac{1}{x}+\frac{1}{y}.$$

Find the value of R if $x = 4\cdot36$ and $y = 2\cdot61$.

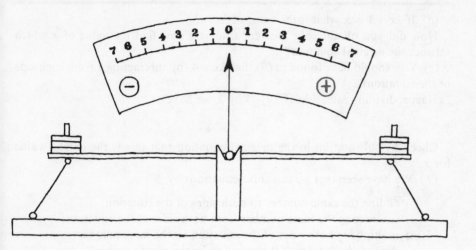

7 Equations and inequalities

1 Solving simple equations

(*a*) Consider the equation $x + 1 = 3$. Use any method to find the value of x. Find the value of x for each of the following:

   (i) $x - 3 = 4$;   (ii) $2x = 4$;   (iii) $\dfrac{x}{2} = 3$.

(*b*) Consider again $x + 1 = 3$.

Subtract 1 from both sides of this equation. Does this method give you the correct value of x? Put $x = 2$ in the equation and check that $x + 1 = 3$ is then a true statement.

Add 3 to both sides of equation (i) and hence find the value of x. Did you obtain the same answer in (*a*)?

What can you do to both sides of the equations (ii) and (iii) to obtain the correct value of x?

(*c*) If $x + a = b$, then

$$x + a - a = b - a$$

so

$$x = b - a.$$

Now find x if (i) $x - a = b$; (ii) $ax = b$; (iii) $\dfrac{x}{a} = b$.

Equations and inequalities

(*d*) If $3x + 1 = 5$, what is the value of $3x$?

How did you obtain your answer? Can you now find the value of x which satisfies the original equation?

(*e*) You should have found in (*d*) that $3x = 4$ (by subtracting 1 from each side of the equation).

Hence, dividing each side of $3x = 4$ by 3, we have

$$x = \tfrac{4}{3}.$$

Check by substitution in the original equation that this is the correct value for x.

(*f*) We have seen that we can solve equations by

  (i) adding the same number to both sides of the equation;
  (ii) subtracting the same number from both sides of the equation;
  (iii) multiplying both sides of the equation by the same number;
  (iv) dividing both sides of the equation by the same number.

This means that if $x = a$ then each of the following are true statements:

  (i) $x + b = a + b$;
  (ii) $x - b = a - b$;
  (iii) $bx = ba$;
  (iv) $\dfrac{x}{b} = \dfrac{a}{b}, b \neq 0$.

(*g*) Can you spot the value of x which satisfies the equation

$$2x + 3 = x + 7?$$

To solve

$$2x + 3 = x + 7$$

we can first subtract x from both sides giving

$$x + 3 = 7$$

and then subtract 3 from both sides giving

$$x = 4.$$

Now solve the equations:

  (i) $3x - 2 = x + 4$; (ii) $2 - x = 2x - 1$.

Exercise A

Solve the following equations and check your answers by substitution.

1 $2x = 5$;	2 $x + 4 = 3$;	3 $x - 1 = {}^-3$;
4 $4 - x = 6$;	5 $5x + 4 = {}^-6$;	6 $3x - 2 = 4$;
7 $\dfrac{x}{4} = {}^-1$;	8 $\dfrac{4}{x} = {}^-1$;	9 $\dfrac{4}{3x} = 4$;

10   $7y + 6 = 3y - 10$;   11 $8y = y + 14$;   12 $7 + x = 9 - 2x$;
13   $2p = 3p + 6$;   14 $8h + 9 = 15 - 4h$;   15 $6 - 2e = 12 - 17e$;
16   $x + 1 = 5x - 7$;   17 $8 - 3n = 2n - 4$;   18 $10z - 5 = 25 - 6z$.

2   The distributive law

We already know that if a, b and c are *counting numbers*, then

$$a \times (b + c) = (a \times b) + (a \times c).$$

For example, the pattern of dots in Figure 1 shows that

$$3 \times (2 + 4) \quad = \quad (3 \times 2) \quad + \quad (3 \times 4)$$

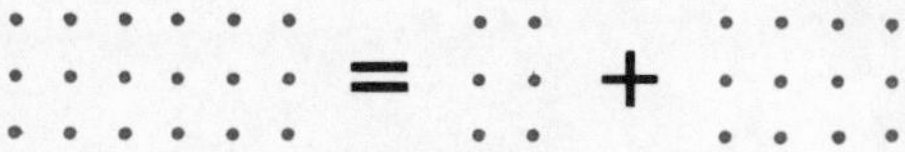

Fig. 1

Multiplication is distributed over addition. We shall now take a closer look at this idea.

(*a*) Work out the following pairs of expressions:

   (i) $3 \times (5 + {}^-2)$, $(3 \times 5) + (3 \times {}^-2)$;
   (ii) $8 \times (\frac{1}{4} + \frac{3}{4})$, $(8 \times \frac{1}{4}) + (8 \times \frac{3}{4})$;
   (iii) ${}^-2 \times ({}^-4 + {}^-1)$, $({}^-2 \times {}^-4) + ({}^-2 \times {}^-1)$;
   (iv) $\frac{1}{2} \times ({}^-3 + 7)$, $(\frac{1}{2} \times {}^-3) + (\frac{1}{2} \times 7)$.

Comment on your results.

(*b*) In fact, no matter what values we choose for a, b and c,

$$a \times (b + c) = (a \times b) + (a \times c).$$

We say that *multiplication is distributive from the left over addition*. Is it true that

$$(b + c) \times a = (b \times a) + (c \times a),$$

no matter what values we choose for a, b and c?

If so, we can say that multiplication is distributive *from the right* over addition.

(*c*) Work out the following pairs of expressions:

   (i) $3 \times (5 - 2)$, $(3 \times 5) - (3 \times 2)$;
   (ii) $8 \times (\frac{3}{4} - \frac{1}{4})$, $(8 \times \frac{3}{4}) - (8 \times \frac{1}{4})$;
   (iii) ${}^-8 \times ({}^-4 - {}^-1)$, $({}^-8 \times {}^-4) - ({}^-8 \times {}^-1)$;
   (iv) $\frac{1}{2} \times ({}^-3 - 7)$, $(\frac{1}{2} \times {}^-3) - (\frac{1}{2} \times 7)$.

We can see that multiplication is distributive *from the left* over subtraction. Is multiplication distributive *from the right* over subtraction?

Equations and inequalities

(*d*) Make two copies of Figure 2. On one shade the region which represents $A \cap (B \cup C)$ and on the other the region which represents $(A \cap B) \cup (A \cap C)$. What can you say about the operations $\cap$ and $\cup$?

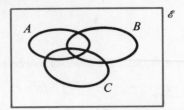

Fig. 2

By drawing two more diagrams, find out whether $\cup$ is distributive from the left over $\cap$.

Exercise B

1 Work out $6 \div (3 + {}^-2)$ and $(6 \div 3) + (6 \div {}^-2)$.

Is division distributive from the left over addition? Do you need to try other triples of numbers in order to be sure?

Now work out $(8 + 4) \div {}^-2$ and $(8 \div {}^-2) + (4 \div {}^-2)$.

Is division distributive from the right over addition? Do you need to try other triples of numbers in order to be sure?

2 Copy the table in Figure 3 and complete it to show whether the first operation is distributive from the left over the second operation.

		Second operation			
		$+$	$\times$	$-$	$\div$
	$+$	No	No	No	No
First	$\times$	Yes			
operation	$-$	No	No	No	
	$\div$	No	No	No	No

Fig. 3

3 Find out whether matrix multiplication is distributive both from the left and from the right over matrix addition.

4 The operations $*$ and $\circ$ are defined on $\{w, r, g\}$ by the following tables:

$*$	w	r	g
w	r	g	w
r	g	w	r
g	w	r	g

$\circ$	w	r	g
w	w	r	g
r	r	w	g
g	g	g	g

Find out whether (i) $*$ is distributive over $\circ$ for $\{w, r, g\}$, (ii) $\circ$ is distributive over $*$ for $\{w, r, g\}$.

5 Investigate whether there are any operations which are distributive over themselves.

3 Using the distributive law

(a) We can use the fact that multiplication is distributive over addition and subtraction to remove brackets. For example:

$$x(x + 3y) = (x \times x) + (x \times 3y)$$
$$= x^2 + 3xy$$

and

$$2(3y - 5) = (2 \times 3y) - (2 \times 5)$$
$$= 6y - 10.$$

Rewrite the following expressions without brackets:

(i) $a(b + c)$;   (ii) $2a(a + b)$;   (iii) $(x + 2)x$;
(iv) $5(2 + 4x)$;   (v) $^-3(2p - 1)$;   (vi) $8(3 - 5k)$.

(b) We can also use the distributive law in the 'opposite direction' to insert brackets. For example:

$$3a + 3b = 3(a + b) \quad \text{and} \quad pq - pr = p(q - r).$$

Writing an expression such as $p^2 + pr$ as $p(p + r)$ is called *factorizing* the expression.

Factorize the following expressions:

(i) $ab + ac$;   (ii) $3y + xy$;   (iii) $4q - pq$;
(iv) $a^2 + ab$;   (v) $2x^2 - 3x$;   (vi) $pq^2 + 2pq$.

(c) We can use the distributive law in 'both directions' to help us to simplify expressions. For example:

$$^-5x + 8x = (^-5 + 8)x$$
$$= 3x$$

and

$$2(x - 3) + 6 = 2x - 6 + 6$$
$$= 2x$$

Simplify:

(i) $^-4y + 11y$;   (ii) $3a - 9a$;
(iii) $2(x + 5) + 2$;   (iv) $6 + 3(u - 2)$;
(v) $3a + (a - 5)$;   (vi) $3(p + 1) + 2(2p + 4)$;
(vii) $3(5 - 2b) + 4(4 + b)$;   (viii) $7(n - 2) + (7n + 1)$.

(d) Now consider the expression $4 - 3(2 + x)$. We can write

$$4 - 3(2 + x) = 4 + {}^{-}3(2 + x)$$
$$= 4 + {}^{-}3.2 + {}^{-}3.x$$
$$= 4 + {}^{-}6 + {}^{-}3.x$$
$$= 4 - 6 - 3x.$$

Notice that the combination of a subtraction and an addition gives a subtraction:

$$4 - 3(2 + x) = 4 - 6 - 3x.$$

In the same way,

$$4 - 3(2 - x) = 4 + {}^{-}3(2 + {}^{-}x)$$
$$= 4 + {}^{-}3.2 + {}^{-}3.{}^{-}x$$
$$= 4 + {}^{-}6 + {}^{+}3x.$$

This shows us that the combination of two subtractions gives us an addition:

$$4 - 3(2 - x) = 4 - 6 + 3x.$$

These results are summarized by the following table:

	+	−
+	+	−
−	−	+

Simplify (i) $^{-}2 \times {}^{-}6$; (ii) $^{-}2 \times {}^{+}6$; (iii) $2 - {}^{-}3$; (iv) $2 - {}^{+}3$; (v) $2 + {}^{-}3$.

Do you agree that the combination table above can be used in all cases when − or ${}^{-}$ is combined with + or ${}^{+}$?

(e) Use the combination table to multiply out (i) $3 - 2(1 - x)$; (ii) $x - 3(2 - x)$; (iii) $2(1 - x) + 4x$; (iv) $2(2 - x) - 3(x - 4)$.

Hence simplify each expression.

(f) We should now be able to solve the equation

$$2(x + 3) + 3(x - 1) = 5.$$

Using the distributive law,

$$2x + 6 + 3x - 3 = 5$$
$$5x + 3 = 5$$
$$5x = 2$$
$$x = \tfrac{2}{5}.$$

Solve the equations:

(i) $x - 3(2 - x) = 4$; (ii) $2(1 - x) + 4x = 0$; (iii) $2(2 - x) - 3(x - 4) = 3x$.

Exercise C

1   Rewrite the following expressions without brackets:

   (a) $4(2u + 3)$;   (b) $^-5(w + 2)$;   (c) $8(2a - 3b)$;
   (d) $^-3(1 - p)$;   (e) $^-p(2 - p)$;   (f) $g(f - g)$;
   (g) $^-h(n^2 + 3)$;   (h) $^-p(4 - 3p)$;   (i) $(k - 1)k$;
   (j) $(a - b - c)a$;   (k) $^-6(a - b - c)$;   (l) $^-x(y - x^2)$.

2   Factorize:

   (a) $3v + uv$;   (b) $2a + 2b$;   (c) $x^2 - 2xy$;
   (d) $pq^2 - qp^2$;   (e) $lmn - mn^2$;   (f) $3mn - 6np$;
   (g) $4p^2 - 2p$;   (h) $3q - 9q^2$;   (i) $ab^3 - a^3b$.

3   Simplify:

   (a) $p + 2 + 3p$;   (b) $5 - s + 4s$;
   (c) $2a - 3b - 5a - b$;   (d) $3x + 4y - 2x - 6y$;
   (e) $a^2 + 2b^2 - a^2 - b^2$;   (f) $7 - x - 5 - 2x$.

4   Simplify:

   (a) $3(a + 1) + 2(a - 3)$;   (b) $4(2k + 3) - 3(k - 4)$;
   (c) $2(m + 5) - (3m + 7)$;   (d) $5(4 - 3c) - 4(5 + 3c)$;
   (e) $2(1 - y) - 3(y - x)$;   (f) $5(1 - 3y) - 2(y - 3)$;
   (g) $3(y - 7) - 7(y + 3)$;   (h) $6(x^2 - 2y) - 2(x^2 + 6y)$.

5   Solve:

   (a) $2(x + 1) + x = 8$;   (b) $3(x - 4) + 2x = 1$;
   (c) $5x - (x + 1) = 11$;   (d) $9x - 2(2x - 8) = 16$;
   (e) $3(b + 1) - 4(b - 1) = 0$;   (f) $2(3y + 1) + 4(y - 1) = ^-7$;
   (g) $4(p - 2) - 3(p - 3) = 0$;   (h) $4(1 - 2s) - 3(3s - 2) = ^-7$;
   (i) $11(k - 2) - (10 + 3k) = 0$;   (j) $2(a - 1) - 3(2 - a) + 4(2a - 5) = ^-2$.

6   Solve for x:

   (a) $3x + 5x = 16$;   (b) $ax + bx = c$ $(a + b \neq 0)$.

4   Further equations

(a) If $\dfrac{y}{5} = 3$, what is the value of y?

If $\dfrac{2x + 4}{5} = 3$, what is the value of $2x + 4$?

You should have found that $2x + 4 = 15$. Now find x. Solve the equations:

   (i) $\dfrac{x - 3}{6} = 2$;   (ii) $\dfrac{2x - 3}{2} = 4$.

(b) If $\dfrac{y}{4} = \dfrac{x}{3}$,

then multiplying both sides by 12,

$$3y = 4x.$$

If $\dfrac{y}{3} = \dfrac{z}{2}$, explain why $2y = 3z$.

(c) Now consider the equation

$$\frac{x+2}{3} = \frac{7-x}{2}.$$

Multiplying both sides by 6 we have

$$2(x+2) = 3(7-x).$$

Hence

$$2x + 4 = 21 - 3x$$
$$5x = 17$$
$$x = \tfrac{17}{5}.$$

Solve the equation

$$\frac{y-4}{3} = \frac{y+6}{7}.$$

Now read through the following examples before you attempt Exercise D.

Example 1

Solve the equation

$$\frac{2x+4}{6} = \frac{3-x}{2}.$$

Multiplying both sides by 12,

$$2(2x+4) = 6(3-x).$$

Using the distributive law,

$$4x + 8 = 18 - 6x.$$

Hence

$$4x + 6x = 18 - 8 \quad \text{(why?)}$$

and simplifying,

$$10x = 10$$
$$x = 1.$$

$$\left(\text{Check}: \frac{2.1+4}{6} = \frac{3-1}{2}, \text{ i.e. } \frac{6}{6} = \frac{2}{2}\right).$$

Example 2

Solve the equation

$$\frac{2x+1}{3} = \frac{3x-1}{4} + 3.$$

Multiplying both sides by 3,

$$2x + 1 = \frac{3(3x-1)}{4} + 9.$$

Multiplying both sides by 4,

$$4(2x + 1) = 3(3x - 1) + 36$$
$$8x + 4 = 9x - 3 + 36$$
$$4 + 3 - 36 = 9x - 8x$$
$$^-29 = x.$$

Hence

$$x = {}^-29.$$

Check that this is the correct answer by substituting $x = {}^-29$ in both sides of the original equation.

Exercise D

Solve the equations 1 to 12. Check that your answers satisfy the equations.

1   $\dfrac{3x-7}{2} = 7;$ 2 $\dfrac{4-x}{3} = 1;$

3   $\dfrac{5-2x}{4} = 7x;$ 4 $5 + x = \dfrac{2x}{3};$

5   $4x - 1 = \dfrac{3x}{2};$ 6 $\dfrac{x+1}{4} = \dfrac{x-2}{3};$

7   $\dfrac{3-2x}{7} = \dfrac{1-x}{5};$ 8 $\dfrac{2x+1}{4} = 2 + \dfrac{x}{3};$

9   $2 - \dfrac{y}{3} = \dfrac{3y+1}{4};$ 10 $3 - \dfrac{x+1}{2} = \dfrac{x-1}{4} + 1;$

11   $\dfrac{a}{3} + \dfrac{a+2}{5} = 1;$ 12 $\dfrac{b}{3} + \dfrac{b}{2} = 1 - \dfrac{b+1}{4}.$

5   Inequalities

(*a*) Since 5 lies to the right of $^-1$ on the number line (see Figure 4), we write

$$5 > {}^-1.$$

Equations and inequalities

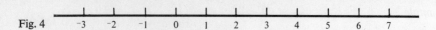

Fig. 4

(b) We have seen that:

    (i) we may add the same number to both sides of an equation;
    (ii) we may subtract the same number from both sides of an equation;
    (iii) we may multiply both sides of an equation by the same number;
    (iv) we may divide both sides of an equation by the same number.

We shall now try to find out what we may do with an inequality.

(c) If we add 2 to both sides of the inequality $5 > {}^{-}1$, we obtain the true statement $7 > 1$ (see Figure 5).

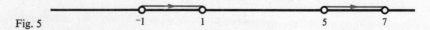

Fig. 5

Add (i) 4; (ii) $^{-}3$; (iii) 7 to both sides of this inequality. Do you obtain a true statement in each case?

Subtract (i) 4; (ii) $^{-}3$; (iii) 7 from both sides of the inequality. Draw diagrams like Figure 5 to represent what you have done.

(d) Now multiply both sides of this inequality by (i) 2; (ii) 3; (iii) 0; (iv) $^{-}1$; (v) $^{-}3$. Do you always obtain a true statement?

Start with a different inequality. In which cases do you obtain a true statement?

(e) You should have found that:

    (i) you may add the same number to both sides of an inequality;
    (ii) you may multiply both sides of an inequality by the same *positive* number;
    (iii) you may multiply both sides of an inequality by the same negative number *provided that you change $>$ to $<$, or $<$ to $>$*.

Figures 6, 7 and 8 should help you to see why this is so.

Adding 2 to both sides of the inequality may be thought of geometrically as a translation through 2 units to the right. If a number a lies to the right of a number b, then $a + 2$ must lie to the right of $b + 2$ and we write

$$a > b \Rightarrow a + 2 > b + 2$$

to mean 'if a is greater than b, then $a + 2$ is greater than $b + 2$'.

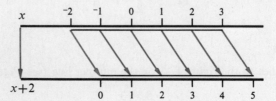

Fig. 6

Explain in the same terms how you might subtract 3 from both sides of the inequality.

(*f*) Multiplying both sides of an inequality by 2 may be thought of geometrically as an enlargement from zero with scale factor 2. Thus multiplication by 2 moves each number twice as far from zero but leaves it on the same side of zero. If a number *a* lies to the right of a number *b*, then 2*a* must lie to the right of 2*b* and we write

$$a > b \Rightarrow 2a > 2b.$$

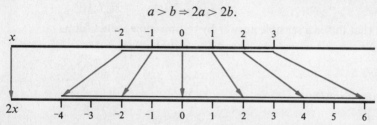

Fig. 7

Multiplying by the negative number ⁻2 may be thought of geometrically as an enlargement from zero with scale factor ⁻2. Thus multiplication by ⁻2 moves each number twice as far from zero and also moves it to the opposite side of zero. If a number *a* lies to the right of a number *b*, then ⁻2*a* must lie to the *left* of ⁻2*b* and we write

$$a > b \Rightarrow {}^-2a < {}^-2b.$$

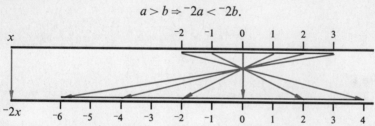

Fig. 8

Provided we remember that the rules for '>' and '<' are more restricted than the rules for '=', we can write solutions for inequalities in much the same way as we do for equations.

Example 3

Solve the inequality

$$2x + 3 > 13.$$

Subtract 3 from both sides,

$$2x > 10.$$

Divide both sides by 2,

$$x > 5.$$

Is this a sensible answer?

Does $x = 5\frac{1}{4}$ satisfy the inequality? Does $x = 4\frac{1}{2}$?

Equations and inequalities

Example 4

Solve the inequality

$$-\tfrac{1}{3}x > {}^{-}8.$$

Multiply both sides by $^{-}3$ and change $>$ to $<$,

$$x < 24.$$

Check that this is a sensible answer by testing some values for x.

Example 5

Solve the inequality

$$^{-}2x \leqslant 7 + 3x.$$

Subtract $3x$ from both sides,

$$^{-}5x \leqslant 7.$$

Divide both sides by $^{-}5$ and change $\leqslant$ to $\geqslant$,

$$x \geqslant {}^{-}\tfrac{7}{5}$$

$$x \geqslant {}^{-}1\tfrac{2}{5}.$$

Exercise E

Solve the inequalities in Questions 1 to 16.

1	$p + 4 > {}^{-}2$;	2	$2q > 10$;
3	$8 \geqslant 1 + u$;	4	$1 < 4 - n$;
5	$3y < {}^{-}42$;	6	$2x + 1 \leqslant 5$;
7	$^{-}4k > 8$;	8	$2(n + 3) < 10$;
9	$3m - 2 > 4$;	10	$\tfrac{1}{2}r \geqslant {}^{-}6$;
11	$^{-}2x + 3 < 7$;	12	$8 - 3k \leqslant 2$;
13	$2p + 3 \geqslant p - 5$;	14	$y + 5 < 3y - 7$;
15	$2(3x + 1) + 4(x - 1) > {}^{-}7$;	16	$4(x - 1) \leqslant 3(x + 5) - 12$.

17 The sum of three consecutive integers is less than 99. If the smallest of these integers is n, what are the other two integers? Write down an inequality involving n and solve it. What can you say about the smallest of the three integers?

18 The sum of the lengths of any two sides of a triangle is greater than the length of the third side. The lengths of the sides of a triangle are 5 cm, 9 cm and x cm. What can you say about x?

19 A scout builds a bridge by nailing together three planks of length 10 m. The bridge must be greater than 20 m but less than 26 m in length if it is to be strong enough to support him. If the overlap between each plank is x m complete the statement: 'the length of the bridge satisfies the inequalities

$$20 < \quad < 26'.$$

Hence find the maximum and minimum overlap he can allow.

Miscellaneous Exercise F

1 Solve:

(a) $n + \frac{1}{2} = 5\frac{1}{2}$;   (b) $9 > 1 - q$;   (c) $^-3y \leqslant 12$;

(d) $1 - x = 2$;   (e) $\dfrac{7}{p} = \dfrac{1}{3}$;   (f) $5 - a > 126$;

(g) $4 \leqslant ^-\frac{1}{3}k$;   (h) $28 = 5b$;   (i) $48 \leqslant \frac{1}{2}(1 + r)$.

2 Solve:

(a) $2x + 5 = 12$;   (b) $2(x + 5) = 12$;

(c) $\dfrac{x + 5}{2} = 12$;   (d) $\dfrac{2}{x + 5} = 12$.

3 Solve:

(a) $4(6 - 2x) = ^-16$;   (b) $2x - 3 < 7$;

(c) $^-3x + 4 \geqslant 10$;   (d) $\dfrac{6}{x} + 2 = 4$;

(e) $8 - \dfrac{6}{x} = 2$;   (f) $7 - 2x \leqslant 4$.

4 Solve:

(a) $2x + 3 = 3x - 4$;   (b) $3a - 2 < a + 4$;
(c) $4 - 2x = 5x + 1$;   (d) $3(x - 4) + 2x = 1$;
(e) $\frac{1}{2}(3x - 2) = ^-4$;   (f) $2(\frac{1}{2}x + 3) = ^-6$;
(g) $\frac{3}{4}(4x - 2) = x$;   (h) $\frac{1}{3}(3 - x) = \frac{1}{4}(1 - x)$;

(i) $\dfrac{1}{x} = \dfrac{7}{x} - 2$;   (j) $4y + 1 = 6y - 8$.

5 (a) Solve the equation $\dfrac{10}{x} = 5$. (b) Solve the inequality $\dfrac{10}{x} > 5$ if (i) $x > 0$,

(ii) $x < 0$. (c) Solve completely: (i) $2 < \dfrac{1}{x}$; (ii) $\dfrac{2}{x} \geqslant \dfrac{1}{x} - 1$.

6 Solve for x:

(a) $px + q = r$;

(b) $p(x + q) = r$;

(c) $\dfrac{x + q}{p} = r$;

(d) $\dfrac{p}{x + q} = r$;

(e) $px + qx = 4$;

(f) $\dfrac{p}{x} + \dfrac{q}{x} = r$.

7 Solve the following equations and check your answer by substitution:

(a) $\dfrac{3x + 7}{5} = \dfrac{1 + 2x}{6}$;

(b) $\dfrac{1 + s}{4} = \dfrac{2s - 1}{2}$;

(c) $\dfrac{1 - 4t}{5} = t + 2$;

(d) $b + \tfrac{1}{7} = 1 - 2b$;

(e) $x - \tfrac{1}{2} = 3 - x$;

(f) $\dfrac{2(3 - x)}{3} = \dfrac{3(2 - x)}{2}$;

(g) $\dfrac{(1 - a)}{3} - \dfrac{(2 - a)}{2} = 1$;

(h) $\dfrac{x - 2}{4} + x = 0$;

(i) $\dfrac{4}{z} + 3 = 6$;

(j) $\dfrac{2}{m} - \dfrac{1}{2m} = 1$;

(k) $\dfrac{1}{x - 1} + \dfrac{2}{3} = 3$;

(l) $\dfrac{p}{3} + \dfrac{p - 1}{4} = p$.

8 Formulas

1 Using formulas

(a) The following table shows a metric equivalent of figures given in the Highway Code:

Speed (v km/h)	40	60	80	100
Stopping distance (d m)	16	36	64	100

Fig. 1

Can you tell, just by looking at the table, the stopping distance for a car travelling at (i) 50 km/h, (ii) 75 km/h?

(b) Use the table to find the values of v^2 when $d = 16, 36, 64$ and 100. Can you now see a connection between v^2 and d? What is it? Write it in the form $d = \ldots$.

(c) You should have written

$$d = \frac{1}{100} v^2 \qquad \text{or} \qquad d = \frac{v^2}{100}.$$

If a car is travelling at 50 km/h, $v = 50$. So, using $d = \dfrac{v^2}{100}$,

$$d = \frac{50^2}{100} = \frac{2500}{100} = 25.$$

Therefore the stopping distance for a car travelling at 50 km/h is 25 m.

Calculate the stopping distance for a car travelling at 75 km/h.

Formulas

(*d*) Now suppose we know the stopping distance and we wish to find the speed.

If the stopping distance of a car is 49 m, $d = 49$ and so

$$49 = \frac{v^2}{100}.$$

Hence

$$v^2 = 4900$$

and

$$v = 70.$$

The speed for a stopping distance of 49 m is therefore 70 km/h.

In fact 4900 has *two* square roots: 70 and $^-70$. Why is $v = {}^-70$ unsuitable here?

(*e*) Calculate the speed for a stopping distance of 69 m. To how many significant figures is it sensible to give the answer? (You will need to use either square root tables or a slide rule.)

(*f*) At what speed is it safe to travel when the visibility is 30 m?

Exercise A

1 $m = \frac{1}{2}(x + y)$.

    (*a*) Find *m* when $x = 6$ and $y = {}^-4$.
    (*b*) Find *x* when $m = {}^-4$ and $y = 2$.

2 $a = 6 - \dfrac{12}{r}$. Find *r* when $a = 8$. $\left(Hint: \text{first find } \dfrac{12}{r} \text{ when } a = 8.\right)$

3 The roasting time for a joint of meat is 45 mins per kg plus 45 minutes extra. If a joint of mass *M* kg takes *T* minutes to roast, write down the formula connecting *T* and *M*.

4 The maximum safe speed for a cyclist riding round a circular track of radius *r* m is *v* km/h, where

$$v = \frac{12}{5}\sqrt{(20r)}.$$

    (*a*) Find the maximum safe speed on a track of radius 5 m.
    (*b*) Find the radius of a track for which the maximum safe speed is 36 km/h.

(*Hint*: first find $\sqrt{(20r)}$ when $v = 36$.)

5 $F = \dfrac{mv^2}{r}$.

    (*a*) Find *F* when $m = 12$, $v = 3$ and $r = 8$.
    (*b*) Find *m* when $F = 15$, $v = 5$ and $r = 10$.
    (*c*) Find *v* when $F = 48$, $m = 4$ and $r = 3$.

6    $T = \dfrac{12}{\sqrt{c}}.$

     (a)   Find T when $c = 64$.

     (b)   Find c when $T = 4$.

7   Figure 2 shows a square garden, each side of which is l m in length. A path of width d m surrounds a central square lawn of side s m.

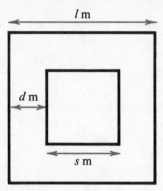

l m

d m

s m

Fig. 2

     (a)   If the total area of the garden is A m², write down a formula connecting A and l.

     (b)   Copy and complete the following formula which connects s, l and d:

$$s = l -$$

     (c)   If the area of the lawn is L m², write down a formula connecting L, d and l.

     (d)   Write down a formula for the cost of seeding the central square with grass seed if the cost is p pence per square metre. Explain any new letters that you use.

     (e)   Write down an expression for the area of the path in terms of l and s. What is the total cost of concreting the path at £t per square metre?

2   The subject of a formula

(a) In section 1, we found that the connection between the speed, v km/h, of a car and its stopping distance, d m, is given by

$$d = \dfrac{v^2}{100}.$$

When this connection is written in the form $d = \ldots$, we say that d is the *subject* of the formula.

By first multiplying both sides of $d = \dfrac{v^2}{100}$ by 100 and then taking the square root of both sides, rearrange the formula so that v is the subject, that is, write it in the form $v = ...$

(b) You should have found that

$$v = \sqrt{(100d)} \qquad \text{or} \qquad v = 10\sqrt{d}.$$

Substitute $d = 49$ in one of these formulas to find the speed of the car when the stopping distance is 49 m. Is your answer the same as the one obtained in section 1(d)?

(c) Copy the following working and complete it to make r the subject of the formula

$$v = \frac{12}{5}\sqrt{(20r)}.$$

Multiplying both sides by $\frac{5}{12}$,

$$\frac{5}{12}v =$$

Squaring both sides,

$$\frac{25}{144}v^2 =$$

Dividing both sides by 20,

$$\frac{1}{20} \cdot \frac{25}{144}v^2 =$$

Since we require r to be the *subject* of the formula, we write

$$r = \frac{5}{576}v^2.$$

(d) Use $r = \frac{5}{576}v^2$ to find r when $v = 36$ and compare your answer with that which you obtained in Exercise A, Question 4(b).

Exercise B

In Questions 1 to 12, make the letter in the bracket the subject of the formula.

1	$A = 3b$	(b)		2	$v = Ik$	(I)
3	$v = u + at$	(t)		4	$m = \frac{1}{2}(x + y)$	(x)
5	$F = \dfrac{mv^2}{r}$	(v)		6	$F = \dfrac{mv^2}{r}$	(r)
7	$d = \sqrt{(11 \cdot 5h)}$	(h)		8	$A = 3(p + 5)$	(p)
9	$v^2 = u^2 + 2as$	(s)		10	$v^2 = u^2 + 2as$	(u)

11   $a = 6 - \dfrac{12}{r}$ (r) 12 $s = \dfrac{u+v}{2}t$ (v)

13   (a) Make c the subject of the formula $T = \dfrac{12}{\sqrt{c}}$. (b) Use your formula to find c (i) when $T = 3$, (ii) when $T = 2 \cdot 4$.

14   The perimeter in centimetres, p, of a rectangle of length l cm and width w cm is given by

$$p = 2(l + w).$$

Make l the subject of this formula and hence find the length of a rectangle whose perimeter is 36 cm and whose width is 7·3 cm.

15   Make l the subject of the formula $T = 2\pi \sqrt{\left(\dfrac{l}{g}\right)}$ and hence find l when $T = 12$ and $g = 10$.

16   The total surface area in square centimetres, S of a cylinder with radius r cm and height h cm is given by

$$S = 2\pi r h + 2\pi r^2.$$

Make h the subject of this formula and hence find the height of a cylinder with surface area 84 cm² and radius 2 cm.

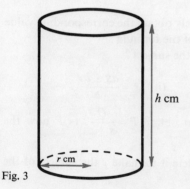

h cm

r cm

Fig. 3

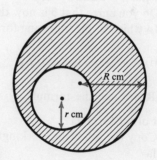

R cm

r cm

Fig. 4

17   A circle of radius r cm is cut from a circle of radius R cm.

     (a)   If the shaded area (see Figure 4) is A cm², give a formula for A in terms of r and R.

     (b)   Calculate A when $r = 2 \cdot 7$ and $R = 4 \cdot 1$.

     (c)   Make R the subject of the formula and hence find R when $A = 2$ and $r = 0 \cdot 8$.

18   Make c the subject of the formula $E = mc^2$ and hence find c when $m = 0 \cdot 03$ and $E = 2 \cdot 7 \times 10^{19}$. Give your answer in standard form.

Formulas

3 Changing the subject of a formula

(a) The formula

$$x = ab + 2b$$

can be rewritten in the form

$$b = \tfrac{1}{2}(x - ab).$$

Is b now the subject of the formula? On putting $x = 5$ and $a = 3$, do you *immediately* obtain the corresponding value of b?

Before reading on, try to rearrange

$$x = ab + 2b$$

so that b *is* the subject of the formula.

(b) Our difficulty is that b occurs in the formula more than once. We can overcome this by using the distributive law to obtain

$$x = b(a + 2).$$

Hence

$$\frac{x}{a + 2} = b$$

and so

$$b = \frac{x}{a + 2}.$$

Now put $x = 5$ and $a = 3$. Do you immediately obtain the corresponding value of b? Do you agree that b is now the subject of the formula?

(c) In which of the following formulas is x the subject?

(i) $x = 3y + 7$;   (ii) $x = 3y^2 - 5x$;   (iii) $x = \dfrac{ax + by}{c}$.

(d) Rearrange the formula $Q + Pt = Ps$ to obtain $P = \dfrac{Q}{s - t}$. Is P now the subject of the formula?

(e) Copy the following working and complete it to make y the subject of the formula

$$x = \frac{3y + 20}{5y}.$$

Multiplying both sides by $5y$,

$$= 3y + 20.$$

Subtracting $3y$ from both sides,

$$= 20.$$

Using the distributive law,

$$y(5x - 3) =$$

118

Dividing both sides by $5x - 3$,

$$y =$$

Exercise C

In Questions 1 to 10 make the letter in the bracket the subject of the formula.

1   $z = 3p + pq$ $\quad\quad$ (p) $\quad\quad\quad$ 2 $s = 2ac + 4ab$ $\quad$ (a)

3   $h = d^2 - 3hR$ $\quad\quad$ (h) $\quad\quad\quad$ 4 $y = \dfrac{x + 5}{x}$ $\quad\quad$ (x)

5   $p = \frac{1}{2}mv^2 - \frac{1}{2}mu^2$ (m) $\quad\quad$ 6 $A = P + \dfrac{Prt}{100}$ $\quad$ (P)

7   $z = \dfrac{x}{x + 2}$ $\quad\quad$ (x) $\quad\quad\quad$ 8 $R = \dfrac{s - 5}{s - 2}$ $\quad\quad$ (s)

9   $v = \dfrac{uf}{u - f}$ $\quad\quad$ (f) $\quad\quad\quad$ 10 $W = \dfrac{2t - 3}{3t - 2}$ $\quad$ (t)

11   We can make h the subject of the formula $S = 2\pi rh + 2\pi r^2$ by the following method:

$$S = 2\pi rh + 2\pi r^2$$
$$S = 2\pi r(h + r)$$
$$\frac{S}{2\pi r} = h + r$$
$$h = \frac{S}{2\pi r} - r.$$

In Exercise B, Question 16, you obtained the formula $h = \dfrac{S - 2\pi r^2}{2\pi r}$.

Explain clearly how this can be rewritten in the form $h = \dfrac{S}{2\pi r} - r$.

12   If $T = \dfrac{3W - a}{2a}$, is it true that $T = \dfrac{3W}{2a} - \frac{1}{2}$?

13   Interpret the formula $V = \pi R^2 h - \pi r^2 h$ and rewrite it making h the subject.

Summary

If a formula is written in the form

$$b = \ldots$$

and b does not occur on the right-hand side, then b is said to be the *subject* of the formula.

Formulas

1   (a) Use the formula $v = 6\sin 15t°$ to help you to complete a copy of the following table:

t	0	1	2	3	4	5	6
v	0		3				

  (b) Plot the graph of $v = 6\sin 15t°$ for values of t from 1 to 6.

2   Make l the subject of the formula $S = \pi r l$ and hence find l when $S = 50$ and $r = 3\cdot2$.

3   Express q in terms of p given that $p = \sqrt{(q - 5)}$.

4   Make r the subject of the formula $R = 2(r - 3)$.

5   w, a, x are positive numbers such that $w^2 = a^2 - a^2 x^2$.

    (a) Find w when $a = 5$ and $x = 0\cdot6$.

    (b) Make x the subject of the formula and hence find x when $w = 5$ and $a = 10$.

    (c) Make a the subject of the formula and hence find a when $w = 9$ and $x = 0\cdot8$.

6   The volume in cubic centimetres, V, of a sphere of radius r cm is given by the formula

$$V = \tfrac{4}{3}\pi r^3.$$

Make r the subject of this formula and hence find the radius of a sphere whose volume is 100 cm³.

7   If $v = w\sqrt{(a^2 + x^2)}$, find w when $v = 72$, $a = 13$ and $x = 5$.

8   Make x the subject of each of the following formulas:

    (a) $y = ax + b$;   (b) $y = p(x + q)$;

    (c) $y + 5x = mx$;   (d) $y = \dfrac{x + k}{2x}$;

    (e) $y = \dfrac{x}{x - c}$;   (f) $y = \dfrac{x + a}{a - x}$.

9   A passenger travelling by air is allowed to take 20 kg of luggage free. For any luggage over this amount the charge is 4p per kg.

If C is the total charge in pence and w is the weight of his luggage in kg where $w > 20$, which of the following formulas is correct?

    (i) $C = 4w - 20$;   (ii) $C = 4(w - 20)$;

    (iii) $C = 20 - 4w$;   (iv) $C = 4(w + 20)$.

10　The cost of building a bridge in concrete is given by

$$c = 20\,000\left(\frac{12}{n} + n\right)$$

where c is the cost in pounds and n is the number of spans.

　　Calculate the values of c when $n = 1, 2, 3, 4, 5, 6$ and enter them in a copy of the following table.

n	c
1	260 000
2	
3	
4	
5	
6	

How many spans should there be if the bridge is to be built as cheaply as possible?

11　Ohm's law states that if a current of I amps flows through a resistance of R ohms then the difference in potential, V volts, across the resistance is given by $V = IR$.

    (a)　If a current of 5 amps flows through a resistance of 480 ohms, what is the voltage difference across the resistance?

    (b)　Make I the subject of the formula.

    (c)　The power consumed, W watts, is given by $W = IV$. Combine the two formulas to find W (i) in terms of I and R; (ii) in terms of V and R.

    (d)　An electric fire consumes 2000 watts and the voltage of the power supply is 250 volts. Find (i) the resistance of the fire, (ii) the current consumed.

12　If $P = 2t - 1$, express t in terms of P. Given also that $Q = 6t + 5$, express Q in terms of P.

13　It is given that

$$\frac{1}{K} = \frac{1}{a} + \frac{1}{b}.$$

    (a)　Find K when $a = 3$ and $b = \frac{1}{2}$.

    (b)　Express K in terms of a and b, giving your answer in its simplest form.

Statistics projects

How many standard shapes of frequency diagrams are there?

(*a*) During the eighteenth century the errors that arose in astronomical observations were investigated. It was found that the errors when graphed formed a bell-shaped curve (see Figure 1).

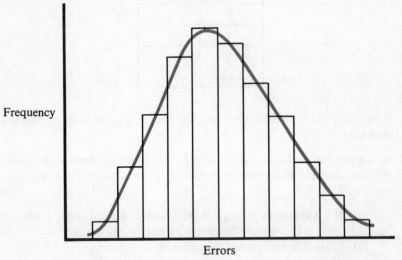

Fig. 1

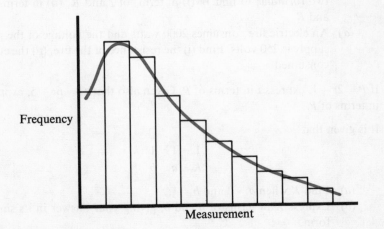

Fig. 2

This curve has a 'hump' and is symmetrical about this hump. We call this standard shape of frequency diagram a NORMAL curve. It arises in symmetrical situations, i.e. when values above and below the mean are equally likely.

(b) Over a hundred years ago a Frenchman, Henri Poisson, investigated another type of standard frequency diagram. It has an early 'hump' and then the values 'tail' off as shown in Figure 2.

This shape of frequency diagram which we call a POISSON curve occurs in science and in situations where observations are taken over equal intervals of time or space.

Now complete some of the projects which follow and find out into which pattern they can be classified, i.e. Normal, Poisson, or other types.

PROJECT	NORMAL	POISSON	OTHER TYPES
1			
2			
3			
.			
.			
.			

Much of the time and labour of these projects can be saved if you do them as a class or group project.

1 Toss a coin 1000 times. Record your results on squared paper putting them in groups of 10 thus:

$$H \quad T \quad H \quad H \quad T \quad T \quad H \quad H \quad T \quad H$$
$$T \quad T \quad T \quad H \quad T \quad H \quad H \quad H \quad T \quad H$$

(a) Go through your results and count the number of heads. Calculate the success fractions for the number of heads and the number of tails. Write these fractions in decimal form.

(b) Now go through the set of 1000 tosses taking them in groups of two, and record the number of 'heads' in each pair. For example,

$$HT \ | \ HH \ | \ HT \ | \ HT \ | \ TH$$
$$TT \ | \ TT \ | \ HT \ | \ TH \ | \ TT$$

Number of heads	Tally marks	Frequency	Success fraction in decimal form
0						
1	ⅢⅠ		
2					

Statistics projects

(c) Repeat the process with groups of 5 recording the number of 'heads' in each group.

(d) Repeat with groups of 10.

(e) Since it is easy to make mistakes when counting, here is a method of checking. Suppose that in the table for groups of 2, there are 267 cases of '1 head', and 115 cases of '2 heads'. The total number of heads in this group is 267 plus 230 which gives 497 heads and this must agree with the number of heads in part (a).

(f) Now draw a graph of the function:

Number of heads → Success fraction (in decimal form)
for groups of 1, 2, 5 and 10.

2 The following project can be done by throwing the die the required number of times for each of the sections, (a) to (d), or by recording the results of the throws for section (a) and using these for (b) to (d). This method is similar to project 1 but you must be very careful to be accurate.

(a) Throw a die 648 times and record the frequency of each number.

(b) Throw two dice 324 times and record the frequency of the total score each time.

(c) Throw two dice 324 times and record the frequency of the difference between the values on the two dice.

(d) Throw three dice 216 times and record the frequency of the total score.

(e) Draw graphs of score → frequency for each of the sections.

3 Measure to the nearest cm the heights of the members of your class and, if possible, several other classes throughout your school. Record your results by grouping your data into 5 cm intervals as follows:

Age 11 *years*

Height in cm	Boys	Girls
140–145		
145–150		
150–155		
.		
.		
.		
.		

Draw up similar tables for the other ages.

Draw a graph of height → frequency for (a) each age group; (b) all the boys; (c) all the girls; (d) all the information.

4 Take a piece of graph paper and draw a line on it as in Figure 3. Drop grains of rice onto this sheet aiming at the thick line. Count the number of grains in cm strips on each side of the line and tabulate your results. Repeat many times. Draw a graph of distance from central line → frequency.

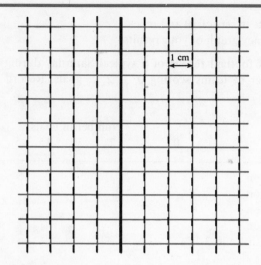

Fig. 3

5   Secure a sheet of graph paper over a dart board; number the squares as shown in Figure 4. Aim at the bull's-eye and record the two numbers which describe the square in which the dart lands. For example the shaded square is recorded as 5, 6. Form a frequency table for the x and y numbers separately.

Draw a graph of (i) x numbers $\rightarrow$ frequency, and (ii) y numbers $\rightarrow$ frequency.

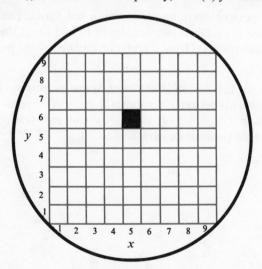

Fig. 4

6   Mark 10 discs with the numbers 1–10. Put them in a box, shake them and take one without looking. Replace and repeat many times, recording the results.

Find the frequency of each number.

Take the results in pairs, and add the numbers in each pair. Form a frequency table for the results (lowest 2, highest 20).

Take the results in sets of 5 and repeat (lowest 5, highest 100).

Take the results in sets of 10 and repeat.
Draw a frequency graph of your results.

7   Take a set of football results of a typical Saturday during the season and count the number of teams scoring 0, 1, 2,... goals. Record your results as shown below.

| | Number of goals | | | | | | |
	0	1	2	3	4	5	...
Division 1							
Division 2							
Division 3							
Division 4							
Scottish 1 and 2							

Draw graphs of score → frequency for each of the groups separately and one graph of all the groups combined.
Take the results in sets of 3 and add them together and record the results.
Draw a graph of total score → frequency.
Now repeat taking sets of 4, 5 matches.

8   Colour dried peas by marking them with a red felt-tip pen. Mix them up with ordinary dried peas. Draw out samples of 10 and count the number of red peas recording your results. Draw a graph of number of red peas in sample → frequency.

9   Obtain a copy of the *Annual Abstract of Statistics* from a library. Look up the tables which give (*a*) personal incomes; (*b*) legitimate live births; (*c*) number of beds available in hospitals; (*d*) deaths by violence; (*e*) further education courses. Draw graphs to illustrate each section.

Revision exercises

Slide rule session no. 3

Give all answers as accurately as your slide rule permits.

1   $23 \times 67 \cdot 8$.   2 $1 \cdot 91 \times 9 \cdot 8$.

3   $2 \cdot 12 \div 1 \cdot 56$.   4 $230 \div 16 \cdot 2$.

5   $\sqrt{39 \cdot 5}$.   6 $\sqrt{395}$.

7   $(1 \cdot 67)^2$.   8 $(16 \cdot 7)^2$.

9   $\dfrac{1 \cdot 23 \times 2 \cdot 31}{3 \cdot 12}$.   10 $(167)^3$.

Slide rule session no. 4

Give all answers as accurately as possible.

1   19×37.   2 $0 \cdot 045 \times 77$.

3   $19 \div 37$.   4 $77 \div 0 \cdot 045$.

5   $19 \times \sqrt{61 \cdot 5}$.   6 $\sqrt{(220 \cdot 5 \times 8)}$.

7   $(0 \cdot 0468)^2$.   8 $\pi \times (8 \cdot 4)^2$.

9   $\dfrac{541 \times 7 \cdot 67}{23}$.   10 $\sqrt{810}$.

Quick quiz no. 3

1   Correct $3 \cdot 1416$ to 2 s.f.

2   If it is Monday, today, what is the probability that it is Tuesday tomorrow?

3   Find the mean of 16, 15, 67, 45, 23, 14.

4   Find the mean of 906, 905, 957, 935, 913, 904 by using the result of Question 3.

5   Find the value of $(a - b)c$ when $a = {}^-3$, $b = 4$ and $c = {}^-2$.

6   Are a square and triangle topologically equivalent?

7   $y = 2 \sin 60°$. Find y.

8   Square the matrix $\begin{pmatrix} 0 & 2 \\ 1 & 1 \end{pmatrix}$.

9   Give the image of the point $(3, {}^-4)$ under a reflection in the line $x + y = 0$.

10   Give the image of the point $({}^-2, 3)$ under the translation $\begin{pmatrix} -3 \\ -4 \end{pmatrix}$.

Revision exercises

Quick quiz no. 4

Give the answers to the following four questions in their lowest terms:

1   $\frac{2}{3} + \frac{3}{4} - \frac{7}{8}$.   2 $\frac{3}{5} \times \frac{10}{11} \times \frac{22}{9}$.   3 $\frac{3}{8} \div \frac{9}{16}$.

4   $(\frac{1}{8} + \frac{1}{4}) - (\frac{3}{16} - \frac{1}{24})$.

5   What regular solid has 6 faces, 12 edges and 8 vertices?

6   Write down the inverse of the function $x \to 3x$.

Carry out the following duodecimal calculations (@ stands for 'ten' and $*$ stands for 'eleven').

7   $1@7 + **3$.   8 $794@ - 487$.

9   $23* \times 1@3$.   10 $69 \div 3$.

Exercise C

1   Write down a set of five integers:

     (a)   whose mean is 5 and whose median is 3;

     (b)   whose median is 5 and whose mean is 3.

2   When p and q are positive numbers, $p * q$ denotes the positive number $\sqrt{(pq)}$. Find the value of $24 * (4 * 9)$.

3   Find the image of the letter V whose vertices are $(2,2)$, $(4, {}^-2)$, $(6,2)$ under the transformation whose matrix is $\begin{pmatrix} 0 & {}^-\frac{1}{2} \\ \frac{1}{2} & 0 \end{pmatrix}$.

4   Find the matrix $\mathbf{X}$ which satisfies each of the following matrix equations:

     (a) $\mathbf{X} + \begin{pmatrix} 1 & 0 \\ 0 & 2 \end{pmatrix} = \begin{pmatrix} 3 & 4 \\ 5 & 6 \end{pmatrix}$;

     (b) $\mathbf{X} + \begin{pmatrix} 2 & 3 \\ {}^-1 & 4 \end{pmatrix} = \begin{pmatrix} 6 & 7 \\ 2 & 3 \end{pmatrix}$;

     (c) $2\mathbf{X} + \begin{pmatrix} 4 \\ 1 \end{pmatrix} = \begin{pmatrix} 8 \\ 5 \end{pmatrix}$;

     (d) $2\mathbf{X} + \begin{pmatrix} 1 \\ 2 \end{pmatrix} = \begin{pmatrix} 6 \\ 0 \end{pmatrix}$;

     (e) $\mathbf{X} + \begin{pmatrix} 1 & 0 & 1 \\ 0 & 1 & 1 \\ 0 & 1 & 2 \end{pmatrix} = \begin{pmatrix} 6 & 7 & 8 \\ 9 & 1 & 0 \\ 2 & 3 & 4 \end{pmatrix}$;

     (f) $3\mathbf{X} + \begin{pmatrix} 2 & 1 & {}^-1 \\ 0 & 2 & 3 \\ 4 & {}^-1 & {}^-2 \end{pmatrix} = \begin{pmatrix} 5 & 7 & {}^-4 \\ 3 & 8 & 0 \\ 4 & 2 & {}^-2 \end{pmatrix}$.

5 'Pirates Cove to Cutlass Creek is $\begin{pmatrix} -1 \\ 2 \end{pmatrix}$. For the gold, start at Pirates Cove, then

$$\begin{pmatrix} 3 \\ 0 \end{pmatrix}, \ \begin{pmatrix} 1 \\ 1 \end{pmatrix}, \ \begin{pmatrix} -2 \\ 1 \end{pmatrix}, \ \begin{pmatrix} 2 \\ 2 \end{pmatrix}, \ \begin{pmatrix} -2 \\ 1 \end{pmatrix}, \ \begin{pmatrix} -1 \\ 1 \end{pmatrix}.$$

Where, if you came across this note, would you look for the treasure on the island in the figure?

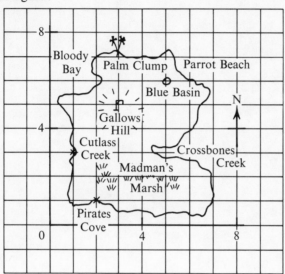

Fig. 1

Exercise D

1 (a) Simplify $A \cap (B \cup B')$. (b) If $E = \{\text{animals}\}$, $D = \{\text{dogs}\}$ and $F = \{\text{fat animals}\}$, write a sentence equivalent to the statement $D \cap F' = \varnothing$.

2 If $\mathbf{B} = \begin{pmatrix} 0 & -1 \\ 1 & 0 \end{pmatrix}$ work out $\mathbf{B}^2$, $\mathbf{B}^3$ and $\mathbf{B}^4$. Describe the transformations represented by $\mathbf{B}$, $\mathbf{B}^2$, $\mathbf{B}^3$ and $\mathbf{B}^4$. What would $\mathbf{B}^6$ and $\mathbf{B}^{17}$ represent?

3 Solve the following equations:
(a) $2(x - 2) = 6$; (b) $2(x - 1) = 7$.

4 P is the point $(1,1)$, Q is the point $(2,2)$ and R is the point $(2,0)$. Transform triangle PQR by each of the following matrices.

(a) $\begin{pmatrix} 1 & 0 \\ 0 & 1 \end{pmatrix}$; (b) $\begin{pmatrix} 1 & 0 \\ 0 & -1 \end{pmatrix}$; (c) $\begin{pmatrix} -1 & 0 \\ 0 & 1 \end{pmatrix}$;

(d) $\begin{pmatrix} 3 & 0 \\ 0 & 3 \end{pmatrix}$; (e) $\begin{pmatrix} 0 & -2 \\ 2 & 0 \end{pmatrix}$.

Describe what has happened to triangle PQR in each case in terms of translation, reflection, rotation and enlargement.

5 (a) Express 0·266 66... correct to three decimal places. (b) Express 0·2666... correct to two significant figures. (c) If $x = 0.266\,666...$ write down the value of $10x$ and from these two values obtain the value of $9x$. Hence express x as a fraction in its simplest terms.

9 Vectors

1 A review

What have (*a*) shopping lists, (*b*) journeys and (*c*) translations in common? The mathematical answer is that they all behave as vectors.

(*a*) The housewife shopping in her local supermarket might have a list of basic items:

$$\begin{array}{ll} \text{tea} & \tfrac{1}{2}\,\text{kg} \\ \text{sugar} & 2\,\text{kg} \\ \text{eggs} & \tfrac{1}{2}\,\text{dozen} \\ \text{butter} & 1\,\text{kg} \end{array} \qquad \text{which could be written} \qquad \begin{pmatrix} \tfrac{1}{2} \\ 2 \\ \tfrac{1}{2} \\ 1 \end{pmatrix}.$$

Does it make sense to combine two shopping lists by adding corresponding amounts:

$$\begin{pmatrix} \tfrac{1}{2} \\ 2 \\ \tfrac{1}{2} \\ 1 \end{pmatrix} + \begin{pmatrix} 0 \\ 1 \\ 1\tfrac{1}{2} \\ 1 \end{pmatrix} = \begin{pmatrix} \tfrac{1}{2} \\ 3 \\ 2 \\ 2 \end{pmatrix}?$$

Does it make sense to multiply a shopping list by a number:

$$3 \times \begin{pmatrix} \tfrac{1}{2} \\ 2 \\ \tfrac{1}{2} \\ 1 \end{pmatrix} = \begin{pmatrix} 1\tfrac{1}{2} \\ 6 \\ 1\tfrac{1}{2} \\ 3 \end{pmatrix}?$$

(b) The home–factory journey ($H \rightarrow F$) on the grid in Figure 1 may be written $\binom{3}{1}$. How would you write the $F \rightarrow W$ and the $H \rightarrow W$ journeys? Do you agree that

$$\binom{3}{1} + \binom{1}{3} = \binom{4}{4} \quad \text{and} \quad 2 \times \binom{3}{1} = \binom{6}{2}?$$

What do these equations mean in terms of the journeys?

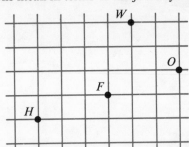

Fig. 1

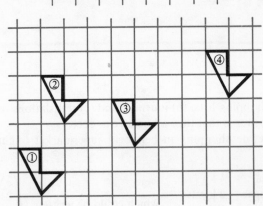

Fig. 2

(c) In Figure 2 ① can be mapped onto ② by the translation $\binom{1}{3}$. How can ② be mapped onto ③? Say what the following mean by referring to the appropriate translations in Figure 2:

$$\text{(i)} \quad \binom{1}{3} + \binom{3}{-1} = \binom{4}{2}; \qquad \text{(ii)} \quad 2 \times \binom{4}{2} = \binom{8}{4}.$$

(d) Quantities which can be added and multiplied by a number according to the rules

$$\text{(i)} \quad \begin{pmatrix} a_1 \\ a_2 \\ a_3 \\ \vdots \end{pmatrix} + \begin{pmatrix} b_1 \\ b_2 \\ b_3 \\ \vdots \end{pmatrix} = \begin{pmatrix} a_1 + b_1 \\ a_2 + b_2 \\ a_3 + b_3 \\ \vdots \end{pmatrix}, \qquad \text{(ii)} \quad k \times \begin{pmatrix} a_1 \\ a_2 \\ a_3 \\ \vdots \end{pmatrix} = \begin{pmatrix} ka_1 \\ ka_2 \\ ka_3 \\ \vdots \end{pmatrix}$$

are called *vectors*.

Exercise A

1 The table shows the sales of an usherette in a cinema:

	Mon	Tues	Wed	Thurs	Fri	Sat	Sun
Ice cream	30	35	36	40	54	77	39
Iced lollies	10	14	12	16	27	55	13
Orange drinks	25	28	30	32	36	66	26
Popcorn	35	35	42	40	45	88	52
Peanuts	15	21	24	24	27	44	26

(a) Express these numbers as column vectors;

(b) rewrite the vectors as simply as possible; e.g.

$$\begin{pmatrix} 4 \\ 6 \\ 8 \\ 10 \end{pmatrix} = 2 \begin{pmatrix} 2 \\ 3 \\ 4 \\ 5 \end{pmatrix};$$

(c) Find the total sales of each item for the week.

2 A translation maps the point $(1,3)$ to the point $(1,7)$. What is the vector of the translation? What are the images of the following points under the same translation: $(3,0)$, $(5,5)$, $(2,^-4)$, $(^-4,2)$, $(0,^-3)$?

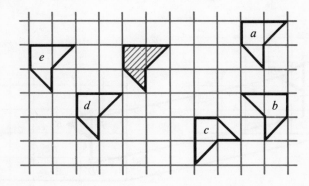

Fig. 3

3 Which of the positions (a), (b), (c), (d), (e) can be reached by a translation of the shaded motif in Figure 3? In each of these cases give the vector of the appropriate translation.

133

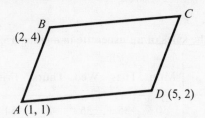

Fig. 4

4 In Figure 4, *ABCD* is a parallelogram. What is **AB** as a column vector? Use it to find the coordinates of *C*. What is **AD** as a column vector? Check that this leads to the same result for the coordinates of *C*.

5 Complete the following. The vector of the translation which maps the point (a, b) to (p, q) is $\begin{pmatrix} p - a \\ ? \end{pmatrix}$.

6 Solve the following equations:

(a) $\begin{pmatrix} x \\ 3 \end{pmatrix} + \begin{pmatrix} 2 \\ y \end{pmatrix} = \begin{pmatrix} 5 \\ 0 \end{pmatrix}$; (b) $\begin{pmatrix} x \\ y \end{pmatrix} + \begin{pmatrix} x \\ y \end{pmatrix} = \begin{pmatrix} {}^-4 \\ 3 \end{pmatrix}$;

(c) $\begin{pmatrix} x \\ y \end{pmatrix} + \begin{pmatrix} 3 \\ x \end{pmatrix} = \begin{pmatrix} 5 \\ 0 \end{pmatrix}$; (d) $p \begin{pmatrix} 3\frac{1}{2} \\ y \\ z \end{pmatrix} = \begin{pmatrix} 10\frac{1}{2} \\ 2\frac{1}{4} \\ y \end{pmatrix}$.

2 Vectors in geometry

(a)

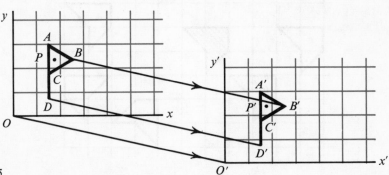

Fig. 5

Figure 5 represents a translation of the (x, y) plane.

What can you say about the line segments *OO'*, *BB'* and *DD'*? The translation can be fully described by any *one* of the directed line segments **OO'**, **BB'** and **DD'**. Can you think of any other way of representing the translation using the letters in the figure?

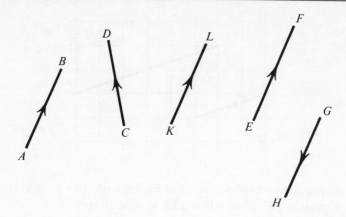

Fig 6

(b) Look at Figure 6. The directed line segments **AB**, **CD**, **KL** and **GH** are equal in length. Which of them are (i) parallel; (ii) marked with arrows pointing in the same direction?

Can you explain why **AB** and **KL** represent the same translation?

How many *different* translations are described in Figure 6?

(c) Any translation is associated with a set of arrowed line segments and it is this *set* which is thought of as the vector which describes the translation. We represent vectors by small letters printed in bold type **a**, **b**, **c** .... You can write these as a̰, b̰, c̰ ....

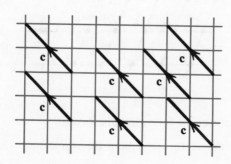

Fig. 7

For example, the directed line segments in Figure 7 all represent the same translation. This vector can be denoted by $\mathbf{c} = \begin{pmatrix} ^-2 \\ 2 \end{pmatrix}$.

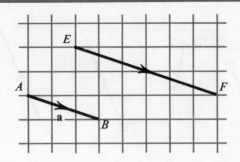

Fig. 8

(d) The two directed line segments in Figure 8 describe parallel translations. If **AB** = **a**, what is **EF**? Write **AB** and **EF** as column vectors.

Exercise B

1 What can you say about the direction and length of line segments labelled?

    (a) **a** and 3**a**;
    (b) ½**b** and **b**;
    (c) 2**c** and 3**c**;
    (d) m**d** and **d**;
    (e) p**e** and q**e**.

2

Fig. 9

Use Figure 9 to answer the following questions:

    (a) What is the vector describing the translation which takes CGHD to KOPL?
    (b) What is the image of the shaded parallelogram under the translation 2**a**?
    (c) What is the image of the shaded parallelogram under the translation 2**a** + **b**?
    (d) What is the vector of the translation taking the shaded parallelogram to OSTP?

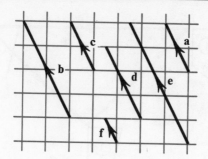

Fig. 10

3   For Figure 10:

(a)   write each of the vectors **b**, **c**, **d**, **e**, **f**, in terms of **a**;
(b)   write each of the vectors **a**, **b**, **c**, **d**, **e**, in terms of **f**.

4

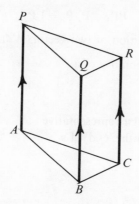

Fig. 11

In Figure 11 **AP**, **BQ**, **CR** are representatives of the same vector. What can you say about the triangles ABC and PQR?

5   (a) If $3\mathbf{a} = (p - 2)\mathbf{a}$, what is the value of p? (b) If $(2q + 3)\mathbf{b} = 4\mathbf{b}$, what is the value of q?

6   Find the values of t, u, v, w in the following:

(a) $t\mathbf{a} = (1 - t)\mathbf{a}$;   (b) $(u + 1)\mathbf{b} = 2u\mathbf{b}$;
(c) $(3 - v)\mathbf{c} = v\mathbf{c}$;   (d) $(w + 3)\mathbf{d} = (2w - 4)\mathbf{d}$.

7   (a) **a** and **b** are vectors with different directions. If $p\mathbf{a} = q\mathbf{b}$, what can you say about p and q? (b) If $(1 - u - v)\mathbf{a} = (v - 2u)\mathbf{b}$ and **a** and **b** have different directions, what are the values of u and v?

3   Adding vectors

In Figure 12 $\mathbf{P}\mathbf{P}_1$ describes the translation mapping ① onto ② and $\mathbf{P}_1\mathbf{P}_2$ the translation mapping ② onto ③.

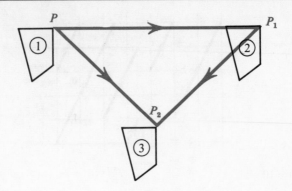

Fig. 12

Consider the single translation mapping ① onto ③. It is represented by $\mathbf{PP_2}$, and so we write:

$$\mathbf{PP_1} + \mathbf{P_1 P_2} = \mathbf{PP_2}.$$

We can represent the addition of two vectors **a** and **b** in the following way:

(a) Choose *any* representative of **a**.

(i)

(b) Choose the particular representative of **b** which starts at the 'end' of **a**.

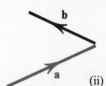

(ii)

(c) Join the 'start' of **a** to the 'end' of **b**. This directed line segment is a representative of **a** + **b**.

Fig. 13

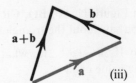

(iii)

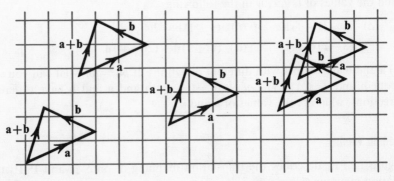

Fig. 14

Figure 14 shows the addition carried out starting with several different representatives of **a**. Do you agree that all the segments labelled **a** + **b** are representatives of the same vector? This means that our definition of vector addition does not depend on which particular representative of **a** we choose.

Exercise C

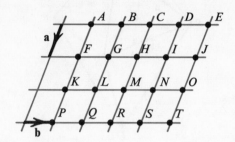

Fig. 15

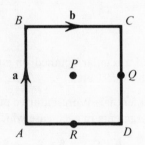

Fig. 16

1 Express the following (see Figure 15) in terms of **a** and **b**: **IJ**, **HM**, **FP**, **QT**, **BH**, **CO**, **AM**, **AL**, **KT**, **FS**.

2 In Figure 16, *ABCD* is a square, *Q* and *R* are mid points of sides and *P* is the centre of *ABCD*. Write the following in terms of **a** and **b**: **AC**, **PC**, **RQ**, **AQ**, **RC**.

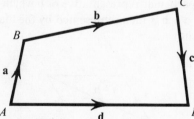

Fig. 17

3 In Figure 17, *ABCD* is a quadrilateral with

$$\mathbf{a} = \begin{pmatrix} 1 \\ 3 \end{pmatrix}, \qquad \mathbf{b} = \begin{pmatrix} 5 \\ 2 \end{pmatrix}, \qquad \mathbf{c} = \begin{pmatrix} 4 \\ -1 \end{pmatrix}.$$

Find **d** as a column vector. What is a special feature of *ABCD*? Check your result by drawing the figure accurately on squared paper.

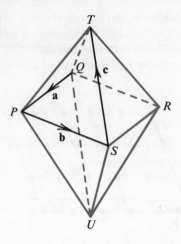

Fig. 18

4   Figure 18 is a drawing of a regular octahedron and it may help you to have
a model to look at for this question.

(i)   Which line segment is a representative of **a** + **b**?
(ii) Find two line segments in each case which are representatives of

$$\mathbf{b} + \mathbf{c}, \qquad \mathbf{a} + \mathbf{c}, \qquad \mathbf{a} + \mathbf{b} + \mathbf{c}.$$

(iii) Which vectors do the line segments **UP**, **PT** and **UT** represent?

5   Look at this alternative definition of vector addition which is based on the
parallelogram rather than the triangle.

(*a*)   Choose any representative of **a**.
(*b*)   Draw the particular representative of **b** which has the same starting
point as **a**. **a** + **b** is then represented by the diagonal of the parallelogram as shown:

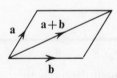

Does this definition depend on the particular representative of **a** which is
chosen first? As in Figure 14, draw several possibilities and look at all the
segments labelled **a** + **b**. Compare again with Figure 14. Does this definition
conflict in any way with the triangle definition?

4 Properties of vector addition

(*a*) Which of the following statements do you agree with?

(*a*) $8 + 7 = 7 + 8$;

(*b*) $9 \times 7 = 7 \times 9$;

(*c*) $9 \div 3 = 3 \div 9$;

(*d*) $(8 - 4) - 1 = 8 - (4 - 1)$;

(*e*) $(4 \times 5) \times 17 = 4 \times (5 \times 17)$;

(*f*) $7 \times (5 + 6) = (7 \times 5) + (7 \times 6)$;

(*g*) $3 + (4 \times 2) = (3 + 4) \times (3 + 2)$.

And what about these?

(*h*) $\begin{pmatrix} 1 & 0 \\ 2 & 1 \end{pmatrix} + \begin{pmatrix} ^-1 & 4 \\ 0 & 3 \end{pmatrix} = \begin{pmatrix} ^-1 & 4 \\ 0 & 3 \end{pmatrix} + \begin{pmatrix} 1 & 0 \\ 2 & 1 \end{pmatrix}$;

(*i*) $\begin{pmatrix} 1 & 2 \\ 1 & 1 \end{pmatrix}\begin{pmatrix} 1 & 0 \\ 1 & 1 \end{pmatrix} = \begin{pmatrix} 1 & 0 \\ 1 & 1 \end{pmatrix}\begin{pmatrix} 1 & 2 \\ 1 & 1 \end{pmatrix}$;

(*j*) $\{3, 4, 5\} \cup \{4, 5, 7\} = \{4, 5, 7\} \cup \{3, 4, 5\}$.

(*b*)

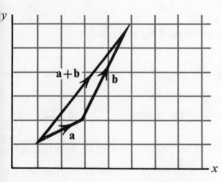

Fig. 19   Fig. 20

If

$$\mathbf{a} = \begin{pmatrix} 2 \\ 1 \end{pmatrix} \quad \text{and} \quad \mathbf{b} = \begin{pmatrix} 2 \\ 4 \end{pmatrix}$$

then

$$\mathbf{a} + \mathbf{b} = \begin{pmatrix} 2 \\ 1 \end{pmatrix} + \begin{pmatrix} 2 \\ 4 \end{pmatrix} = \begin{pmatrix} 4 \\ 5 \end{pmatrix}.$$

(see Figure 19).

Copy Figure 20 and mark in the vector $\mathbf{b} + \mathbf{a}$. Express $\mathbf{b} + \mathbf{a}$ as a column vector. What do you notice about $\mathbf{a} + \mathbf{b}$ and $\mathbf{b} + \mathbf{a}$?

(c) Verify by drawing diagrams similar to Figures 19 and 20 that

(i) $\begin{pmatrix} 2 \\ 1 \end{pmatrix} + \begin{pmatrix} 3 \\ -1 \end{pmatrix} = \begin{pmatrix} 3 \\ -1 \end{pmatrix} + \begin{pmatrix} 2 \\ 1 \end{pmatrix}$;

(ii) $\begin{pmatrix} 0 \\ 4 \end{pmatrix} + \begin{pmatrix} 3 \\ 0 \end{pmatrix} = \begin{pmatrix} 3 \\ 0 \end{pmatrix} = \begin{pmatrix} 0 \\ 4 \end{pmatrix}$.

Do you agree that vector addition is commutative?
(d)

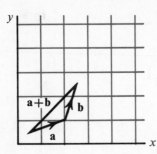

Fig. 21   Fig. 22

Figure 21 shows three vectors **a**, **b** and **a** + **b**.
In Figure 22, the vector triangle has been enlarged by scale factor 2.
Notice that $2(\mathbf{a} + \mathbf{b}) = 2\mathbf{a} + 2\mathbf{b}$.

(e) If $\mathbf{a} = \begin{pmatrix} 1 \\ 1 \end{pmatrix}$ and $\mathbf{b} = \begin{pmatrix} 2 \\ -1 \end{pmatrix}$, work out **a** + **b**, 5**a** and 5**b**. Now find (i) 5**a** + 5**b**;
(ii) 5(**a** + **b**). Do you agree that $5(\mathbf{a} + \mathbf{b}) = 5\mathbf{a} + 5\mathbf{b}$?

(f) Explain with the aid of diagrams like Figures 21 and 22 why $k(\mathbf{a} + \mathbf{b}) = k\mathbf{a} + k\mathbf{b}$.

(g) Draw a diagram to represent the vector (i) 2**a**, (ii) 3**a**, (iii) (2 + 3)**a**. What do you notice? Is it true that $k\mathbf{a} + l\mathbf{a} = (k + l)\mathbf{a}$?

Exercise D

1 Write the following vector expressions in other ways:

(a) $2\mathbf{a} + \mathbf{a}$;   (b) $3\mathbf{a} + 2(\mathbf{a} + \mathbf{b})$;
(c) $2(2\mathbf{a} + \mathbf{b}) + 3(\mathbf{a} + 2\mathbf{b})$;   (d) $(p - 1)\mathbf{a} + (p + 1)\mathbf{a}$;
(e) $(m + n)\mathbf{a} + (n - m)\mathbf{a}$;   (f) $(p + 1)\mathbf{b} + 2\mathbf{b}$.

2 In Figure 23 $\mathbf{AC} = \mathbf{a}$, $\mathbf{CB} = \mathbf{b}$ and $\mathbf{AP} = \frac{1}{3}\mathbf{AB}$. Write in terms of **a**, **b**: **AB**, **AP**, **PB**. Check your results by showing that $\mathbf{AP} + \mathbf{PB} = \mathbf{AB}$.

3 $\mathbf{a} = \begin{pmatrix} a_1 \\ a_2 \end{pmatrix}$, $\mathbf{b} = \begin{pmatrix} b_1 \\ b_2 \end{pmatrix}$. Complete by filling in the blanks:

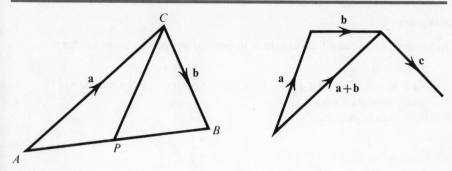

Fig. 23   Fig. 24

(a) $p\mathbf{a} = \begin{pmatrix} pa_1 \\ \end{pmatrix}$;   (b) $q\mathbf{b} = \begin{pmatrix} \\ qb_2 \end{pmatrix}$;

(c) $p\mathbf{a} + q\mathbf{b} = \begin{pmatrix} pa_1 \\ \end{pmatrix} + \begin{pmatrix} \\ \end{pmatrix} = \begin{pmatrix} +qb_1 \\ \end{pmatrix}$;

(d) $p(\mathbf{a} + \mathbf{b}) = p\begin{pmatrix} \\ a_2 + b_2 \end{pmatrix} = \begin{pmatrix} \\ pa_2 \end{pmatrix}$.

4   If $\mathbf{a} = \begin{pmatrix} a_1 \\ a_2 \end{pmatrix}$, show that $(p + q)\mathbf{a} = p\mathbf{a} + q\mathbf{a}$.

5   On a copy of Figure 24 draw a representative of $\mathbf{b} + \mathbf{c}$. Show also a representative of $(\mathbf{a} + \mathbf{b}) + \mathbf{c}$. Is this line segment a representative of $\mathbf{a} + (\mathbf{b} + \mathbf{c})$ as well?

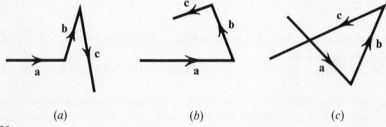

(a)   (b)   (c)

Fig. 25

6   Repeat the stages of Question 5 starting with diagrams similar to those in Figure 25.

7   Make some three-dimensional balsa wood models of three 'nose to tail' vectors $\mathbf{a}$, $\mathbf{b}$ and $\mathbf{c}$ (you should not be able to lay your models flat on the table). Carry out the stages of Question 5 again. Does that same line represent both $(\mathbf{a} + \mathbf{b}) + \mathbf{c}$ and $\mathbf{a} + (\mathbf{b} + \mathbf{c})$?

8   Does the evidence of Questions 5–7 suggest that vector addition is associative?

Vectors

Summary

In general, vector addition has these important properties among others:

$$\mathbf{a} + \mathbf{b} = \mathbf{b} + \mathbf{a}$$
$$(\mathbf{a} + \mathbf{b}) + \mathbf{c} = \mathbf{a} + (\mathbf{b} + \mathbf{c}) \qquad (\mathbf{a}, \mathbf{b}, \mathbf{c} \text{ are vectors}; p, q \text{ are numbers})$$
$$p(\mathbf{a} + \mathbf{b}) = p\mathbf{a} + p\mathbf{b}$$
$$(p + q)\mathbf{a} = p\mathbf{a} + q\mathbf{a}$$

5 Position vectors

If vectors are being used in a graphical situation, the representatives of those vectors which have the origin as their starting points are particularly important. These special representatives are called *position vectors*.

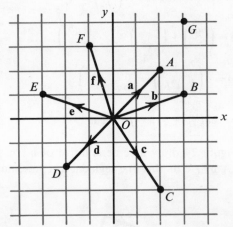

Fig. 26

The line segments **a**, **b**, **c**, **d**, **e** and **f** in Figure 26 are the position vectors of the points A, B, C, D, E and F.

Write the position vector of G as a column vector. What are the coordinates of G?

There is a simple connection between the coordinates of a point and its position vector written in column form: the point with coordinates (x, y) has position vector $\begin{pmatrix} x \\ y \end{pmatrix}$.

We can think of a position vector as a description of a journey starting at the origin and we can transform position vectors by matrices.

For example,

$$\begin{pmatrix} 3 & 0 \\ 0 & 2 \end{pmatrix} \begin{pmatrix} 1 \\ 3 \end{pmatrix} = \begin{pmatrix} 3 \\ 6 \end{pmatrix}$$

i.e. the position vector $\begin{pmatrix} 1 \\ 3 \end{pmatrix}$ is transformed into the position vector $\begin{pmatrix} 3 \\ 6 \end{pmatrix}$ by the matrix

144

$$\begin{pmatrix} 3 & 0 \\ 0 & 2 \end{pmatrix}.$$

What does the position vector $\begin{pmatrix} -2 \\ 4 \end{pmatrix}$ become when transformed by this matrix?

Exercise E

1   What do $\begin{pmatrix} 5 \\ 5 \end{pmatrix}, \begin{pmatrix} 1 \\ 0 \end{pmatrix}, \begin{pmatrix} 0 \\ 1 \end{pmatrix}$ become when they are transformed by

$$\begin{pmatrix} 3 & 0 \\ 0 & 2 \end{pmatrix}?$$

2   Write down a 2 by 4 matrix consisting of the position vectors of A, B, C, D (Figure 27). Multiply it on the left by

$$\begin{pmatrix} 3 & 0 \\ 0 & 2 \end{pmatrix}.$$

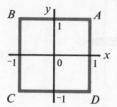

Fig. 27

Show on a diagram $ABCD$ and its image. Can you describe the transformation which

$$\begin{pmatrix} 3 & 0 \\ 0 & 2 \end{pmatrix}$$

represents?

3   Copy and complete the following:

(a) $\begin{pmatrix} 2 & 0 \\ 0 & 2 \end{pmatrix}\begin{pmatrix} 1 \\ 0 \end{pmatrix} = $ \hspace{1cm} ; (b) $\begin{pmatrix} 0 & 1 \\ 1 & 0 \end{pmatrix}\begin{pmatrix} 1 \\ 0 \end{pmatrix} = $ \hspace{1cm} ;

(c) $\begin{pmatrix} 2 & 3 \\ 1 & 2 \end{pmatrix}\begin{pmatrix} 1 \\ 0 \end{pmatrix} = $ \hspace{1cm} ; (d) $\begin{pmatrix} a & b \\ c & d \end{pmatrix}\begin{pmatrix} 1 \\ 0 \end{pmatrix} = $ \hspace{1cm} .

Look carefully at your answers and describe what you notice.

4   Transform the position vector $\begin{pmatrix} 0 \\ 1 \end{pmatrix}$ by each of the matrices in Question 3.

What do you notice if you compare the transformed vectors and the corresponding matrix?

6 Physical vectors

The following information is received in the traffic control room at Heathrow:

Flight No. 683 (B.O.A.C. from Athens)
Time: 10.18
Position: Latitude 51°25′N; Longitude 0°17′E
Height: 4000 m
Speed: 800 km/h

What important fact is missing?

The flight controller needs to know the precise directions in which the aircraft are flying if he is to guide them to a safe landing.

Velocity describes both speed *and* direction so the flight controller must have full details about the positions and velocities of the planes for which he is responsible. Positions and speeds are not sufficient.

Have you seen a light aircraft flying as in Figure 28?

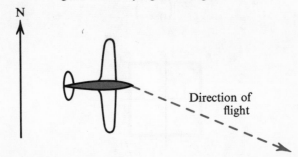

Fig. 28

A plane attempting to fly due east in a strong north-easterly wind would do this.

Suppose the aircraft (capable of a speed of 360 km/h in still conditions) is blown off course by a wind blowing at 90 km/h. How should we combine these two velocities, 360 km/h due east and 90 km/h from the north-east, to obtain the actual velocity of the plane?

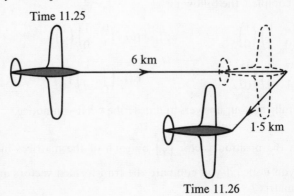

Fig. 29   Time 11.26

The dotted outline in Figure 29 shows where the plane would have been at 11.26 if it had been flying in still air. (360 km/h is the same as 6 km/min.) Its actual position at 11.26 is as shown. This suggests that we can regard the velocities as vectors and add them in the usual way to obtain the actual velocity of the plane (see Figure 30).

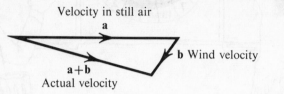

Velocity in still air
a

b Wind velocity

a+b

Fig. 30   Actual velocity

Velocity is therefore a vector quantity; it has size and direction and two velocities can be added according to our definition of vector addition.

Exercise F

1   Which of the following do you consider likely to be vector quantities: temperature, mass, weight, acceleration, time?

2   Draw an accurate scale diagram to find the actual velocity (speed and bearing) of the plane described in the preceding section. A diagram like Figure 29 but based on a one hour interval would be suitable.

3   A canoeist is able to paddle at a speed of 10 km/h in still water. He attempts to paddle straight across a river flowing at 6 km/h. Draw a sketch showing vectors representing these two velocities and his actual velocity. Calculate his speed and the direction in which he travels.

4   Add the velocity vectors 15 km/h bearing 135° and 10 km/h bearing 225° (remember to give both speed and bearing in your answer).

10 Statistics

1 Consistency

(a) Three darts players were having an argument about who was the better player. They recorded their scores as follows:

TOM   54, 45, 52, 26, 30, 20, 61, 40, 32, 42, 38.

DICK   58, 9, 34, 71, 41, 52, 10, 54, 41, 34, 36.

HARRY   24, 44, 53, 16, 24, 142, 24, 4, 64, 30, 15.

They decided that one way in which they could settle the argument was to work out their mean scores. (If you do this, you will find that their mean scores are, in fact, the same.) Tom decided that the only way they could decide was therefore to find out who was the most *consistent* player. There are several ways of doing this:

(i) Compare the *range* of scores. These are given in the table below:

Range

Tom	61–20 = 41
Dick	71–9 = 62
Harry	142–4 = 138

These suggest that Tom's scores were the least widely spread and therefore that he is more consistent than the other two. However, there is an important objection to this measure of spread. The highest and lowest scores might well be looked

148

upon as 'freak' scores. What we are more interested in is the way in which the scores appear to 'cluster' around the mean score. We can therefore calculate

(ii) the *interquartile* range.

If we arrange Tom's scores in order from the lowest to the highest (see Figure 1) then the 'middle score' is 40. Notice that if there are n scores then the middle score is the $\frac{n+1}{2}$ th score. This is known as the *median* score.

What are the median scores for Dick and Harry?

The median divides the data into two halves. Continuing this process we can divide the data into four equal parts. In this case the points of division are called *quartiles*.

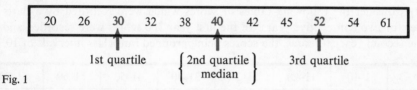

Fig. 1

We can see from Figure 1 that the 1st quartile for Tom's scores is 30, the 2nd quartile (the median) 40 and the 3rd quartile 52. Notice that the 1st quartile is the $\frac{11+1}{4}$ th score, the median the $2\frac{(11+1)}{4}$ th score and the 3rd quartile the $3\frac{(11+1)}{4}$ th score.

Work out the quartiles for Dick's and Harry's scores.

The *interquartile* range is defined as the difference between the values of the 1st and 3rd quartiles. The interquartile range for Tom's scores is $52 - 30 = 22$. Calculate the interquartile range for Dick's and Harry's scores. The value of the interquartile range can be taken as a measure of the spread of the data. This measure has the advantage that it is relatively unaffected by abnormal values (unlike the range as a measure of spread). On this evidence do you agree that Dick is the most consistent darts player?

(*b*) Suppose that Tom records 60 with his next throw so that his scores are now as follows:

20	26	30	32	38	40	42	45	52	54	60	61
1	2	3	4	5	6	7	8	9	10	11	12

Fig. 2

The median score, being the middle value, now has to be taken as the average of 40 and 42, that is 41.

If we used the expression $\frac{n+1}{2}$ to help us find the median score, we would find that we should take the $\dfrac{12+1}{2} = 6\frac{1}{2}$th score! It is obviously nonsense to talk about a $6\frac{1}{2}$th score and this is why we find the value which is midway between the 6th and 7th scores.

Similarly, when we try to find the 1st quartile by using the expression $\dfrac{n+1}{4}$, we find that we should take the $\dfrac{12+1}{4}$th $= 3\frac{1}{4}$th score. We therefore find the score which is $\frac{1}{4}$ of the way between the 3rd and 4th score, i.e. $30\frac{1}{2}$. Use this method to find the 3rd quartile.

(c) Dick scored 150 with his next throw. Use the method of section (b) to find the quartiles for his new range of values. Hence find the interquartile range.

(d) Consider the following tables of scores which were recorded by a darts player for two consecutive years. In the first year 500 scores were recorded and in the second year 50 scores, the scores being grouped into class intervals of 10.

Score	1–10	11–20	21–30	31–40	41–50	51–60	61–70
Frequency	4	10	40	90	140	95	50
Score	71–80	81–90	91–100	101–110	111–120	121–130	131–140
Frequency	34	18	7	4	4	3	1

Score	1–10	11–20	21–30	31–40	41–50	51–60	61–70
Frequency	1	3	6	8	12	6	4
Score	71–80	81–90	91–100	101–110	111–120	121–130	131–140
Frequency	3	2	4	0	0	1	0

Fig. 3

To find the quartiles for the grouped data we can proceed as before. For the first quartile we need to find the $\dfrac{500+1}{4} = 125\frac{1}{4}$th score. However, since we do not know the actual scores, our ultimate answer will only be approximate. It therefore seems reasonable for us to take the first quartile as the 125th score. Check that this score lies in the class interval 31–40.

The first score in the 31–40 class interval is the 55th, and since we want the 125th score we need to find the score which is $\dfrac{125-55}{90} = \dfrac{70}{90} = \dfrac{7}{9}$ths of the 'distance' into this class interval.

Hence the first quartile is approximately $31 + \frac{7}{9} \times 10 \approx 39$.

Use the same method to find the quartiles for the scores in the second year.

(e) Alternatively we can find the quartiles by using a cumulative frequency curve. Consider again the problem of finding the quartiles for the first year's scores. We can proceed as follows:

Score	Frequency	Cumulative frequency	Score	Frequency	Cumulative frequency
1–10	4	4	71–80	34	463
11–20	10	14	81–90	18	481
21–30	40	54	91–100	7	488
31–40	90	144	101–110	4	492
41–50	140	284	111–120	4	496
51–60	95	379	121–130	3	499
61–70	50	429	131–140	1	500

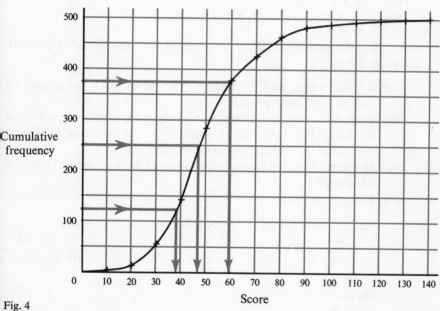

Cumulative frequency

Fig. 4

Notice that the cumulative frequencies are plotted at the ends of the class intervals so as to include all the members of that interval.

To find the first quartile we need to know the 125th score. This is shown by the graph to be approximately 39.

Use the graph to find the second and third quartiles. Hence find the inter-quartile range.

(f) Draw a cumulative frequency curve for the scores in the second year and use your graphs to find the interquartile range.

In which year do you think the darts player was most consistent?

Statistics

Exercise A

1 For the following sets, make out a table showing:

the range,
the median,
the lower quartile,
the upper quartile,
the interquartile range.

   (*a*) {3, 5, 7, 8, 9, 10, 12};

   (*b*) {6, 8, 11, 12, 13, 13, 14, 15, 17, 18, 21};

   (*c*) {154, 157, 159, 160, 174};

   (*d*) {4, 5, 7, 9, 10, 11, 13, 17};

   (*e*) {1·6, 2·3, 4·5, 6·7, 7·1, 7·4, 8·5};

   (*f*) {3, 4, 4, 5, 6, 6, 8, 9, 9, 10};

   (*g*) {3·9, 4·2, 5·7, 6·9};

   (*h*) {3, 6, 9, 10, 11, 12, 4, 6, 6, 7, 8, 6, 12}.

2 Using the information you have collected during the statistics projects answer the following:

   (*a*) Are the means and the interquartile ranges of all the groups in Project 1 the same as each other?

   (*b*) In Project 3 are the means and interquartile ranges of each class the same? If not, how do they differ? Do the heights of boys vary more than the heights of girls of the same age?

   (*c*) In Project 5 are the interquartile ranges of the *x*-scores and *y*-scores the same?

   (*d*) Using your results from Project 7 set them out as shown below:

Number of goals

	0	1	2	3	4	5	6	7	8	9	10	Total matches
Division 1												
Division 2												
Division 3												
Division 4												
Scottish 1 and 2												

Find the median score and the quartiles of each group. Are the interquartile ranges for each of the four divisions significantly different? Are the interquartile ranges of the English teams greater than those of the Scottish?

3 The distribution of ages in a small town is given in the table below. Draw a cumulative frequency diagram and estimate the median and quartile ages.

Ages	Frequency	Ages	Frequency
0–9	809	50–59	698
10–19	796	60–69	504
20–29	667	70–79	295
30–39	707	80–89	97
40–49	715	90 and over	4

4 The table shows the distribution of marks of 648 candidates in a GCE mathematics examination.

Mark	10	20	30	40	50	60	70	80	90	100
Number of candidates who scored less than this mark	8	34	104	190	310	450	543	615	638	648

Draw a cumulative frequency graph to show these data. Use a graph to estimate:

(i) how many candidates scored less than 75 marks;
(ii) the pass mark, if 60% of the 648 candidates passed;
(iii) how many candidates fail to pass by one mark.

5 In an examination the candidates took two papers each marked out of 100.

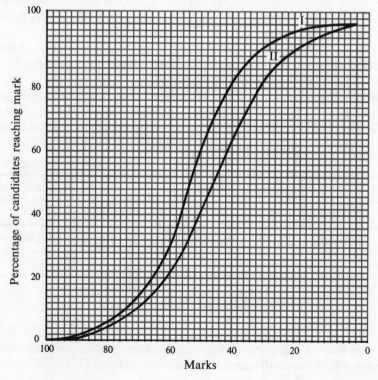

Fig. 5

The diagram shows the cumulative frequency curves for the results of each paper.

  (i) Estimate the median mark for each paper.

  (ii) Estimate the interquartile range for each paper.

  (iii) State with a reason which paper the candidates found more difficult.

  (iv) A candidate obtained 52 marks for Paper I but missed Paper II.

      (a) What percentage of candidates did no better than him on Paper I?

      (b) Suggest what mark he could reasonably be given for Paper II.

2 Class intervals

When collecting data we are concerned with recording observations which in many cases are numerical, for example the heights of people, the number of people living in a certain area, etc. The observations of a particular experiment, or a survey, are known as the POPULATION.

Dart scores are necessarily whole numbers. This is an example of DISCRETE data. Give some other examples of populations which are discrete.

Lengths of leaves are not necessarily whole numbers. Such measurements could form an example of CONTINUOUS data. Can you think of other examples of continuous data?

(a) You have already seen that it is more convenient to group large amounts of data into equal class intervals. A good working rule is to have about 10 class intervals covering the whole range of observations.

In the discrete cases, the data can be grouped easily into classes as shown in the frequency table for darts scores (see Figure 6). Notice that to avoid leaving gaps between 10 and 11, 20 and 21, etc., we change the end points of our groups so that they become $\frac{1}{2}$–$10\frac{1}{2}$, $10\frac{1}{2}$–$20\frac{1}{2}$, ..., $130\frac{1}{2}$–$140\frac{1}{2}$.

Score	$\frac{1}{2}$–$10\frac{1}{2}$	$10\frac{1}{2}$–$20\frac{1}{2}$	$20\frac{1}{2}$–$30\frac{1}{2}$	$30\frac{1}{2}$–$40\frac{1}{2}$	$40\frac{1}{2}$–$50\frac{1}{2}$	$50\frac{1}{2}$–$60\frac{1}{2}$	$60\frac{1}{2}$–$70\frac{1}{2}$
Frequency	4	10	40	90	140	95	50
Score	$70\frac{1}{2}$–$80\frac{1}{2}$	$80\frac{1}{2}$–$90\frac{1}{2}$	$90\frac{1}{2}$–$100\frac{1}{2}$	$100\frac{1}{2}$–$110\frac{1}{2}$	$110\frac{1}{2}$–$120\frac{1}{2}$	$120\frac{1}{2}$–$130\frac{1}{2}$	$130\frac{1}{2}$–$140\frac{1}{2}$
Frequency	34	18	7	4	4	3	1

Fig. 6

(b) Here is another example of discrete data. The population of the number of goals scored in the football league on a particular Saturday is as follows:

Number of goals	0	1	2	3	4	5
Frequency	12	16	9	7	3	1

Fig. 7

A diagram of the results looks like Figure 8.

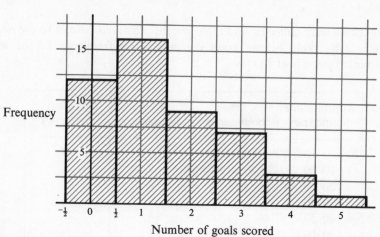

Fig. 8

Number of goals scored

Notice that the number of goals scored is placed at the mid-point of the class interval, and that the bar representing the 1 goal class stretches from $\frac{1}{2}$ to $1\frac{1}{2}$.

It is important to note that the 0 goal class stretches from $-\frac{1}{2}$ to $+\frac{1}{2}$.

(c) *The continuous case.* Suppose a sample of leaves of a particular tree have been collected and the lengths of the leaves measured correct to the nearest millimetre. The information has to be grouped into class intervals of 10 mm. The class intervals could become 0–10, 10–20, 20–30, 30–40, etc., covering the complete range of observations.

In which class do you place a measurement of 20 mm? As the measurements are correct to the nearest millimetre a value of 20 mm could have come from a leaf measuring 19·5 mm or 20·4 mm so we are in doubt into which class it should be placed. Before reading on, make a list of the possible methods of deciding in which class to place this measurement.

Here are some of the ways:

(1) Toss a coin to decide; if heads, then place into the 10–20 group; if tails, then place into the 20–30 group.

(2) Count the number of 20 mm measurements in the total number of observations and then divide them equally between the two classes.

(3) Change the wording of the class intervals to avoid any ambiguity, e.g. the classes become 0–under 10, 10–under 20, ... etc.

(4) Examine the accuracy of the measurements and change the class boundaries to a greater degree of accuracy. The values are measured

155

Statistics

correct to the nearest millimetre so that by changing the class intervals to $^-0\cdot5$–$9\cdot5$, $9\cdot5$–$19\cdot5$, ... etc., no observations will lie on a class boundary.

After the boundaries have been changed it is useful to check that the intervals are of the same width by subtracting the lower boundary from the upper boundary.

Example 1

Seventy leaves were collected and their lengths measured correct to the nearest millimetre. The table below shows the cumulative frequency of the leaves grouped into intervals of 10 mm.

Approximate boundaries	True boundaries	Frequency	Cumulative frequency
0–10	$^-0\cdot5$–$9\cdot5$	0	0
10–20	$9\cdot5$–$19\cdot5$	7	7
20–30		10	
30–40		7	
40–50		14	
50–60		11	
60–70		7	
70–80		7	
80–90		4	
90–100		2	
100–110		1	

Copy and complete the table above. By drawing a cumulative frequency graph calculate the median, quartiles and interquartile range.

Exercise B

1 In an examination two groups of boys obtained the following marks:

Group *A*

```
10  27  19  24  23  18  18  20  11  19  19  17  17  23  15  17
25  14  23  22  27  22  11  28  23  25  19  18  14  10  27  25
27  26  16  17  15  20  21  26  18  14
```

Group *B*

```
23  22  25  28  27  27  20  14  25  21  29  27  27  26  24  26
24  23  29  19  29  29  22  26  25  28  24  27  28  23  29  27
20  29  26  26  19  29  27  28  25  28  27  28  27  30  20  24
22  25  26  29  28  18  21  20  28
```

Choose suitable class intervals, make a frequency table and compare the two groups graphically.

2 On a particular day, the temperatures at 12 noon, measured to the nearest degree C, at thirty places in Europe were:

27 11 20 19 18   5 21 24 14 11 10 20 19 15 18 12
16 11 13   8 21   6 14 21 22 14   4 18 25   9

By taking suitable class intervals show this information graphically.

3 The number of hours of sunshine in Britain, measured correct to the nearest 0·1 of an hour, as given in a daily newspaper are as follows:

8·9 8·2 6·0 6·1 3·6 4·7 4·2 4·3 5·6 2·8 4·2 2·5 2·9 4·5
5·7 7·5 5·9 5·2 6·0 2·7 8·0 6·3 7·5 6·9 6·1 6·6 6·8 5·2
8·0 4·5 3·5 8·2 5·4 11·2 7·7 9·6 8·5 6·9 7·5 1·2

Draw a diagram to illustrate this information. Calculate the average number of hours of sunshine in Britain on that particular day.

4 The points scored by 35 Rugby Union teams on one Saturday were:

13 20   5 18   6 14 20 14 41   6 11 21   6 29   9 47 12
 9 13 20 14   9   3 20 14 13 23 24   6 15   8 24 23   8

Calculate the average number of points scored correct to one decimal place. Group the data into classes and draw a diagram to illustrate the information. By using the middle value of the class calculate the average number of points. Compare the two averages.

5 The data below show the length of a wing of 35 male Passeres measured correct to the nearest millimetre.

Male   75 78 74 73 77 72 74 72 73 73 78 74 78 75
Passeres   77 74 73 76 75 79 76 77 78 77 74 76 76 76
           75 76 75 74 73 74 74

Group the data into suitable classes and draw a graph of the observations. Calculate the average wing length correct to one decimal place. Calculate the median and inter-quartile range.

The wing lengths of 50 female Passeres are shown below.

Female   68 72 71 70 71 71 72 70 70 70 72 72 72 70 73 70 71 74
Passeres   72 71 74 73 74 73 73 75 73 72 74 73 73 69 69 71 72 70
           73 71 71 71 74 73 73 73 72 74 72 73 70 69

Again group these data into classes and illustrate graphically. Calculate the average wing length correct to one decimal place. Calculate the median and interquartile range.

Now combine both sets of results together to form the population of the wing lengths of Passeres. Draw a graph of these results, and calculate the average wing length, median, and interquartile range. Comment on your results.

3 Random selection

(a) When a prize for a raffle is chosen, the tickets are placed into a hat, or a drum, and thoroughly shaken. Then someone, without looking, selects the winning ticket.

In this process each ticket has an equal chance of being selected. We call this a *random* process.

Give some other methods of obtaining random selection.

(b) Statistics is often called the science of large numbers. We cannot say definitely what will happen in a particular event; but we can use statistics to make a prediction about the outcomes of a large number of events.

For example, if an unbiased die is rolled 2400 times, how many times would you expect a 3 to occur?

(c) Statistics has played a very important role in the development of certain sections of biology and other sciences. It also plays a major part in the planning of the country in years ahead, e.g. estimating the number of vehicles and the number of houses that there are likely to be in the year 2000.

If you interview 10 people in your class and discover that 9 of them like a particular pop star you cannot then say that 90% of *all* teenagers like this pop star. If, however, 1000 or 5000 teenagers chosen at random were asked about this particular pop star, you would be able to assess his popularity with more certainty.

The predictions made about the outcome of events when a large amount of information is available are more valid than those made from a small amount of data.

Take a look at the letters on this page. They appear to be randomly distributed. If you closed your eyes and placed a pin point on the page could you say with certainty which letter would be nearest to it?

(d) Make a frequency count of the letters on this page. It will be helpful if you list the letters of the alphabet down the side of a sheet of paper and use tally marks to check them off. It will be easiest if you work in pairs; one to call out, the other to record.

Tally mark	Frequency	Success fraction in decimal form
A		
B		
⋮		
Z		

(e) Calculate the success fraction of the occurrence of each letter. Write your success fraction in decimal form and compare with the decimals shown below.

(f) Repeat for other pages in this book and in other books. It may help to divide some of this work between the members of the class. For very large samples the following success fractions have been obtained:

$E - 0{\cdot}13$ $T - 0{\cdot}09$ $A, O - 0{\cdot}08$ $N, I - 0{\cdot}07$ $S, R - 0{\cdot}06$
$H - 0{\cdot}05$ $L, D - 0{\cdot}04$ $C, U, F - 0{\cdot}03$ $M, P, W, Y - 0{\cdot}02$ $B, G, V - 0{\cdot}01$
$K, Q, X, J, Z - 0{\cdot}005$

Would you say that letters on a page are distributed at random?

Exercise C

1   The following message is in code; every letter has been replaced by another letter. The punctuation and spaces have been omitted

Q M V L Q F X P F R M P Q M R J Y Q J Z D J L P
Y L V G N W E J P E X E A T J Z D J L P G G Q M
J L J R Q M P T J Q M V L Q F A E J R P T J O J
D L W P L F P G A E J U M V K M M P Q M Q U J E
Q F J V S M Q V E O V E J Q V G G G J P Y F J P
L S V T J R V Q Q U J E Q F E V E J

Make a frequency count. You should now be able to identify two letters using the success fractions in (f). Find the most common *pair* of letters. With a little trial and error you should be able to decode the passage.

2   Find out what the letters of the word ERNIE (in the context of premium bonds) mean.

3   If you had been asked to find out how the people in England would react to a new 'drinking and driving' law, how would you select which people to interview? Remember that you must obtain a random sample.

4   If you throw two dice simultaneously a large number of times what success fractions would you expect to obtain for each possible total (2–12)?

11 Matrices and transformations

1 Base vectors

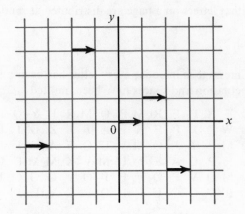

Fig. 1

(*a*) Figure 1 shows several representatives of the vector $\begin{pmatrix} 1 \\ 0 \end{pmatrix}$. This is a vector of unit length in the positive direction of the x axis.

Draw a diagram to show some representatives of the vector $\begin{pmatrix} 0 \\ 1 \end{pmatrix}$. This is a vector in the positive direction of the y axis. What is its length?

(*b*) Express as a single vector, that is, work out:

(i) $3\begin{pmatrix} 1 \\ 0 \end{pmatrix}$;

(ii) $4\begin{pmatrix} 0 \\ 1 \end{pmatrix}$;

(iii) $3\begin{pmatrix} 1 \\ 0 \end{pmatrix} + 4\begin{pmatrix} 0 \\ 1 \end{pmatrix}$.

Do you agree that $\begin{pmatrix} 3 \\ 4 \end{pmatrix}$ can be expressed as a combination of the vectors $\begin{pmatrix} 1 \\ 0 \end{pmatrix}$ and $\begin{pmatrix} 0 \\ 1 \end{pmatrix}$?

(*c*) Figure 2 shows some representatives of the vector $\begin{pmatrix} 5 \\ 2 \end{pmatrix}$.

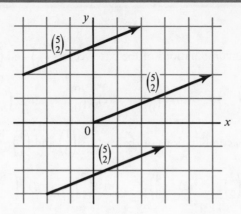

Fig. 2

Look carefully at Figure 3 and then try to express the vector $\begin{pmatrix} 5 \\ 2 \end{pmatrix}$ as a combination of the unit vectors $\begin{pmatrix} 1 \\ 0 \end{pmatrix}$ and $\begin{pmatrix} 0 \\ 1 \end{pmatrix}$.

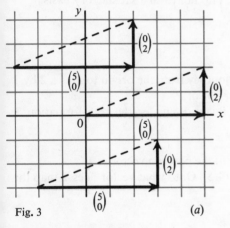

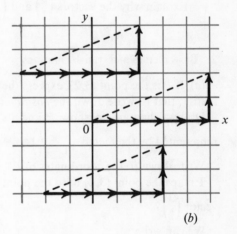

Fig. 3   (a)   (b)

(d) Did you find that

$$\begin{pmatrix} 5 \\ 2 \end{pmatrix} = \begin{pmatrix} 5 \\ 0 \end{pmatrix} + \begin{pmatrix} 0 \\ 2 \end{pmatrix} = 5\begin{pmatrix} 1 \\ 0 \end{pmatrix} + 2\begin{pmatrix} 0 \\ 1 \end{pmatrix}?$$

Now express these vectors as combinations of the unit vectors $\begin{pmatrix} 1 \\ 0 \end{pmatrix}$ and $\begin{pmatrix} 0 \\ 1 \end{pmatrix}$:

(i) $\begin{pmatrix} 3 \\ 7 \end{pmatrix}$;   (ii) $\begin{pmatrix} 4 \\ -3 \end{pmatrix}$;   (iii) $\begin{pmatrix} -2 \\ 5 \end{pmatrix}$;   (iv) $\begin{pmatrix} -6 \\ -1 \end{pmatrix}$;   (v) $\begin{pmatrix} x \\ y \end{pmatrix}$.

Are there any 2 by 1 vectors which cannot be expressed in this way?

The vectors $\begin{pmatrix} 1 \\ 0 \end{pmatrix}$ and $\begin{pmatrix} 0 \\ 1 \end{pmatrix}$ are called *base vectors* because they form a basis from which *all* 2 by 1 vectors can be built.

Matrices and transformations

Exercise A

1 Express as combinations of the base vectors $\begin{pmatrix} 1 \\ 0 \end{pmatrix}$ and $\begin{pmatrix} 0 \\ 1 \end{pmatrix}$:

    (a) $\begin{pmatrix} 8 \\ -5 \end{pmatrix}$;   (b) $\begin{pmatrix} 7 \\ 0 \end{pmatrix}$;   (c) $\begin{pmatrix} 0 \\ 0 \end{pmatrix}$;   (d) $\begin{pmatrix} a \\ b \end{pmatrix}$.

2 Express as combinations of the vectors $\begin{pmatrix} 1 \\ 0 \end{pmatrix}$ and $\begin{pmatrix} 1 \\ 1 \end{pmatrix}$:

    (a) $\begin{pmatrix} 2 \\ 2 \end{pmatrix}$;   (b) $\begin{pmatrix} 4 \\ 3 \end{pmatrix}$;   (c) $\begin{pmatrix} 2 \\ 1 \end{pmatrix}$;   (d) $\begin{pmatrix} -5 \\ -3 \end{pmatrix}$.

Do you think that the vectors $\begin{pmatrix} 1 \\ 0 \end{pmatrix}$ and $\begin{pmatrix} 1 \\ 1 \end{pmatrix}$ form a satisfactory basis from which all 2 by 1 vectors can be built?

Explain why the vectors $\begin{pmatrix} 0 \\ 1 \end{pmatrix}$ and $\begin{pmatrix} 0 \\ 3 \end{pmatrix}$ do not form a satisfactory basis.

2 Base vectors and transformations

(a) If P is the point $(3, 2)$, express the journey from the origin to P as a 2 by 1 matrix, that is, write down the *position vector* of P.

Draw a diagram to show P and its image P' under the transformation $\mathbf{T}$ represented by the matrix $\begin{pmatrix} 2 & {}^-1 \\ 1 & 1 \end{pmatrix}$.

Write down (i) the coordinates of P'; (ii) the position vector of P'.

$\mathbf{T}$ maps the point $(3, 2)$ onto the point $(4, 5)$. Onto what vector does $\mathbf{T}$ map the vector $\begin{pmatrix} 3 \\ 2 \end{pmatrix}$?

We can write

$$\mathbf{T} : \begin{pmatrix} 3 \\ 2 \end{pmatrix} \rightarrow \begin{pmatrix} 2 & {}^-1 \\ 1 & 1 \end{pmatrix} \begin{pmatrix} 3 \\ 2 \end{pmatrix}$$

or

$$\begin{pmatrix} 3 \\ 2 \end{pmatrix} \overset{\mathbf{T}}{\rightarrow} \begin{pmatrix} 4 \\ 5 \end{pmatrix}.$$

(b) What are the images of the base vectors $\begin{pmatrix} 1 \\ 0 \end{pmatrix}$ and $\begin{pmatrix} 0 \\ 1 \end{pmatrix}$ under $\mathbf{T}$? Express $\begin{pmatrix} 3 \\ 2 \end{pmatrix}$ as a combination of $\begin{pmatrix} 1 \\ 0 \end{pmatrix}$ and $\begin{pmatrix} 0 \\ 1 \end{pmatrix}$. Check that $\begin{pmatrix} 4 \\ 5 \end{pmatrix}$ is the *same* combination of the images of $\begin{pmatrix} 1 \\ 0 \end{pmatrix}$ and $\begin{pmatrix} 0 \\ 1 \end{pmatrix}$ under $\mathbf{T}$ (see Figure 4).

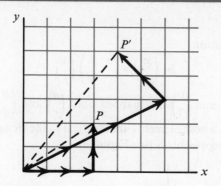

Fig. 4

(c) Look again at the images of $\begin{pmatrix}1\\0\end{pmatrix}$ and $\begin{pmatrix}0\\1\end{pmatrix}$ under **T**.

What is the connection between these images and the columns of the matrix which represents **T**?

What are the images of $\begin{pmatrix}1\\0\end{pmatrix}$ and $\begin{pmatrix}0\\1\end{pmatrix}$ under the transformation represented by

the matrix $\begin{pmatrix}a & b\\c & d\end{pmatrix}$?

(d) What matrix represents the transformation which maps $\begin{pmatrix}1\\0\end{pmatrix}$ to $\begin{pmatrix}1\\2\end{pmatrix}$ and

$\begin{pmatrix}0\\1\end{pmatrix}$ to $\begin{pmatrix}-2\\3\end{pmatrix}$? If you have difficulty, look again at your answers to (c).

(e) We can make use of base vectors to help us to find the matrix which describes a given transformation. Copy and complete the following example.

Example 1

Find the matrix which represents a half-turn about the origin, O.

A half-turn about O maps $\begin{pmatrix}1\\0\end{pmatrix}$ onto $\begin{pmatrix}-1\\0\end{pmatrix}$ and $\begin{pmatrix}0\\1\end{pmatrix}$ onto $\begin{pmatrix}0\\\end{pmatrix}$.

Therefore the required matrix is $\begin{pmatrix}-1 & 0\\ & \end{pmatrix}$.

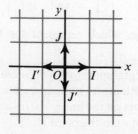

Fig. 5

Matrices and transformations

Summary

Under the transformation

$$S: \begin{pmatrix} x \\ y \end{pmatrix} \rightarrow \begin{pmatrix} a & b \\ c & d \end{pmatrix} \begin{pmatrix} x \\ y \end{pmatrix}$$

the base vectors $\begin{pmatrix} 1 \\ 0 \end{pmatrix}$ and $\begin{pmatrix} 0 \\ 1 \end{pmatrix}$ are mapped onto $\begin{pmatrix} a \\ c \end{pmatrix}$ and $\begin{pmatrix} b \\ d \end{pmatrix}$, that is, they are mapped onto vectors whose elements are identical to the elements in the columns of the matrix which represents S (see Figure 6).

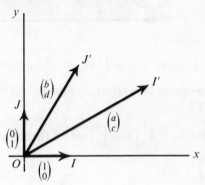

Fig. 6

Exercise B

1   Draw diagrams to show the images of the base vectors

$$\begin{pmatrix} 1 \\ 0 \end{pmatrix} \quad \text{and} \quad \begin{pmatrix} 0 \\ 1 \end{pmatrix}$$

under the transformations represented by the following matrices:

(a) $\begin{pmatrix} 1 & 0 \\ 0 & -1 \end{pmatrix}$;   (b) $\begin{pmatrix} 2 & 0 \\ 0 & 2 \end{pmatrix}$;   (c) $\begin{pmatrix} 2 & -1 \\ 1 & 2 \end{pmatrix}$;   (d) $\begin{pmatrix} -3 & 0 \\ -1 & 2 \end{pmatrix}$.

Which point remains invariant under all four transformations? Does it also remain invariant under the transformation represented by $\begin{pmatrix} a & b \\ c & d \end{pmatrix}$?

2   By finding the images of the base vectors

$$\begin{pmatrix} 1 \\ 0 \end{pmatrix} \quad \text{and} \quad \begin{pmatrix} 0 \\ 1 \end{pmatrix},$$

write down the matrices which represent the following transformations:

(a) reflection in $x = 0$;
(b) anticlockwise rotation through $90°$ about the origin;
(c) enlargement with centre $(0,0)$ and scale factor $\frac{1}{2}$;
(d) shear with points on the line $x = 0$ invariant and such that the point $(1,0)$ is mapped onto the point $(1,1)$.

164

3   Figure 7 shows the unit square $OIAJ$ and its image $OI'A'J'$ under a number of transformations. Find the matrix which represents each of these transformations.

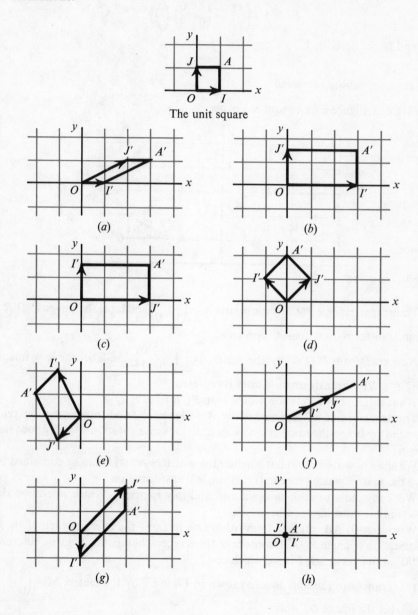

The unit square

Fig. 7

4   Find the images of the base vectors $\begin{pmatrix}1\\0\end{pmatrix}$ and $\begin{pmatrix}0\\1\end{pmatrix}$ under the transformation

$$\mathbf{U}: \begin{pmatrix}x\\y\end{pmatrix} \rightarrow \begin{pmatrix}2&0\\0&3\end{pmatrix}\begin{pmatrix}x\\y\end{pmatrix}$$

and hence describe **U**.

3   Transformations combined

(a) Copy Figure 8 on to squared paper.

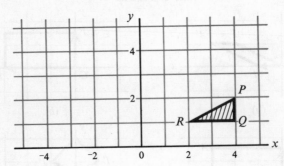

Fig. 8

Transform triangle PQR by the matrix $\mathbf{A} = \begin{pmatrix}0&1\\1&0\end{pmatrix}$ and label the image $P'Q'R'$. What transformation does **A** represent?

Now transform $P'Q'R'$ by the matrix $\mathbf{B} = \begin{pmatrix}-1&0\\0&1\end{pmatrix}$ and label the new image $P''Q''R''$. What transformation does **B** represent?

What single transformation would map PQR onto $P''Q''R''$?

The transformation represented by **A** followed by the transformation represented by **B** has the same effect as an anticlockwise rotation of 90° about the origin.

We shall now try to find out whether the matrices **A** and **B** can be combined to give the matrix which represents this single transformation.

We know how to add, subtract and multiply matrices. Which operation do you think is most likely to be helpful?

Work out (i) **AB**, (ii) **BA**. Draw diagrams to show the effect of each of these matrices on triangle PQR. Do either of them represent an anticlockwise rotation of 90° about the origin? If so, which one?

(b) Transform the unit square shown in Figure 7 by the matrix $\mathbf{M} = \begin{pmatrix}2&1\\0&1\end{pmatrix}$ and label the image $OI'A'J'$.

Now transform $OI'A'J'$ by the matrix $\mathbf{N} = \begin{pmatrix}-1&1\\1&2\end{pmatrix}$ and label the new image $OI''A''J''$.

166

Work out **NM** to obtain a new matrix. Draw a diagram to show the effect of this new matrix on *OIAJ*.

What do you notice?

(*c*) Transform the unit square by the matrix **N** and then transform the image by the matrix **M**.

What single matrix do you think would take the original unit square to the final shape? Check to see whether you are right.

(*d*) Compare your answers to (*b*) and (*c*). Do **MN** and **NM** represent the same transformation? Does **MN** = **NM**?

Summary

If the transformation represented by a matrix **A** is followed by the transformation represented by a matrix **B**, then the combined transformation is represented by **BA**.

Exercise C

1. $\mathbf{A} = \begin{pmatrix} 1 & 1 \\ 0 & 1 \end{pmatrix}$ and $\mathbf{B} = \begin{pmatrix} 1 & 1 \\ -1 & 2 \end{pmatrix}$. Draw the image of the unit square under the transformation represented by **A** and then draw the image of the new shape under the transformation represented by **B**. By multiplying two matrices, find the matrix which takes the unit square to the final shape. Check, by drawing, that your answer is correct.

2. (*a*) $\mathbf{M} = \begin{pmatrix} -1 & 0 \\ 0 & 1 \end{pmatrix}$ and $\mathbf{Q} = \begin{pmatrix} 0 & -1 \\ 1 & 0 \end{pmatrix}$. Evaluate the products **MQ** and **QM**.

   (*b*) Describe clearly the transformation represented by each of the four matrices.

3. The following products of matrices correspond to the combination of two transformations:

   (i) $\begin{pmatrix} 0 & 1 \\ -1 & 0 \end{pmatrix} \begin{pmatrix} 0 & -1 \\ -1 & 0 \end{pmatrix};$ (ii) $\begin{pmatrix} 2 & 0 \\ 0 & 1 \end{pmatrix} \begin{pmatrix} 1 & 0 \\ 0 & 2 \end{pmatrix};$ (iii) $\begin{pmatrix} 1 & 0 \\ 1 & 1 \end{pmatrix} \begin{pmatrix} 1 & 0 \\ 2 & 1 \end{pmatrix}.$

   (*a*) Describe the transformations in each case and find, by drawing, the *single* transformation to which they are equivalent.

   (*b*) Work out the matrix products and check that they correspond to the single transformations which you found in (*a*).

4. Given that

   $$\mathbf{P} = \begin{pmatrix} 1 & 0 \\ 2 & 1 \end{pmatrix}, \qquad \mathbf{Q} = \begin{pmatrix} 4 & -2 \\ 2 & 0 \end{pmatrix}, \qquad \mathbf{R} = \begin{pmatrix} 3 & 1 \\ 2 & 1 \end{pmatrix} \quad \text{and} \quad \mathbf{S} = \begin{pmatrix} 4 & -6 \\ 2 & -2 \end{pmatrix}$$

   investigate the effect of the transformations represented by **QP** and **SR**.

What do you find?

Is the same true for the transformations represented by **PQ** and **RS**?

5 (a) Describe a sequence of three single transformations which will map the unit square $OIAJ$ onto the rectangle $OI'A'J'$ shown in Figure 9.

(b) Find a matrix description of the *simple* transformation which maps $OIAJ$ onto $OI'A'J'$ by combining the three matrices which represent the transformations in (a).

(c) Check that your answer to (b) is correct by considering what happens to the base vectors **OI** and **OJ**.

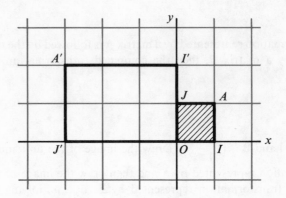

Fig. 9

6 A transformation **T** consists of an enlargement followed by a rotation, both with centres at the origin. If **T** maps $\begin{pmatrix} 1 \\ 0 \end{pmatrix}$ onto $\begin{pmatrix} 4 \\ 3 \end{pmatrix}$, what is:

(a) the image of the vector $\begin{pmatrix} 0 \\ 1 \end{pmatrix}$;

(b) the scale factor of the enlargement;

(c) the angle of the rotation;

(d) the matrix which represents **T**?

12 Area of irregular shapes

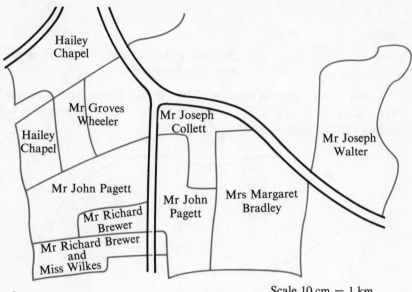

Hailey
Chapel

Mr Groves
Wheeler

Hailey
Chapel

Mr John Pagett

Mr Richard
Brewer

Mr Richard Brewer
and
Miss Wilkes

Mr Joseph
Collett

Mr John
Pagett

Mrs Margaret
Bradley

Mr Joseph
Walter

Fig. 1   Scale 10 cm = 1 km

1 Estimating areas

(*a*) The map illustrates some Enclosures near Chipping Norton in 1770. Copy the map onto squared paper, and, by counting squares, try to discover who owns most land and who owns least. Notice that some people own more than one Enclosure.

(*b*) Figure 2 shows Mrs Bradley's Enclosure divided into simple shapes.

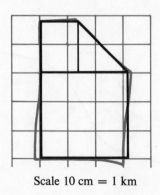

Fig. 2   Scale 10 cm = 1 km

Area of irregular shapes

Calculate the area of each shape and hence estimate in km² the amount of land she owns.

Now use the same method to find the area of land owned by Mr Collett. Is it possible to use this method to obtain a reasonable estimate of the area of any shape?

Exercise A

1 By tracing the map shown at the beginning of this chapter onto squared paper calculate the area of land owned by Mr John Pagett.

2 Grass seed is to be sown at the rate of 60 g/m² (grams per square metre) to make a lawn (see Figure 3). Find the approximate area of the proposed lawn and hence the quantity of grass seed required.

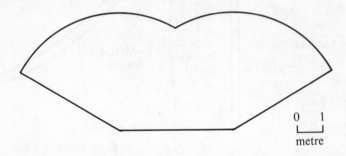

0   1
metre

Fig. 3

3 A builder intends to build houses on a plot of land with each house and garden occupying 350 square metres. The diagram below shows the plot of land. Calculate the area of the land and the number of houses that can be built.

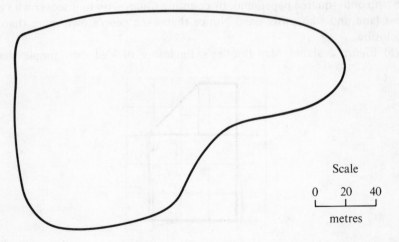

Scale

0   20   40

metres

Fig. 4

170

2 Area of a trapezium

(*a*)

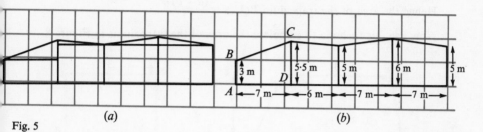

Fig. 5　　　　　　　(*a*)　　　　　　　　　　　　(*b*)

Figure 5 shows an end view of a warehouse. We could divide the shape into rectangles and triangles (see Figure 5*a*), or into trapeziums (Figure 5*b*). Use Figure 5*a* to calculate the area of the shape.

(*b*)

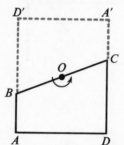

Fig. 6

Now consider Figure 6 which shows the trapezium *ABCD* in Figure 5*b*. Figure 6 shows that if the trapezium is given a half turn about the mid-point, *O*, of *BC* we obtain a rectangle *A'D'AD*. What are the lengths of *AD* and *AD'*? What is the area of the rectangle? You should now be able to deduce that the area of the trapezium is 29·75 m².

Now calculate the areas of the remaining trapeziums in Figure 5*b* and hence find the area of the end of the warehouse. Check that your answer agrees with that which you obtained in section (*a*).

(*c*)

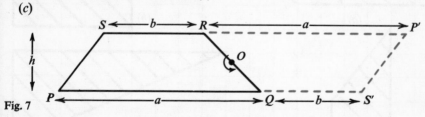

Fig. 7

Figure 7 shows a trapezium *PQRS* which has been given a half turn about the mid-point, *O*, of *RQ*. What kind of quadrilateral is *PS'P'S*?

You will remember that the area of a parallelogram is given by multiplying

171

Area of irregular shapes

the length of the base by the height.

Taking PS' as the base of $PS'P'S$ we can see that the area of the parallelogram is $(a+b)h$.

Hence the area of the trapezium $PQRS$ is $\dfrac{(a+b)h}{2}$.

Now use this formula to calculate the area of the trapeziums in Figure 8.

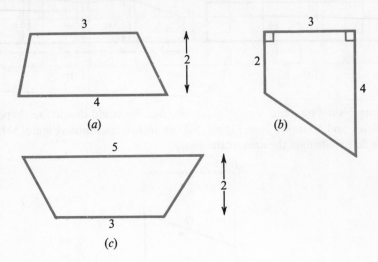

Fig. 8

Exercise B

1 Find the area of the shaded trapeziums in Figure 9.

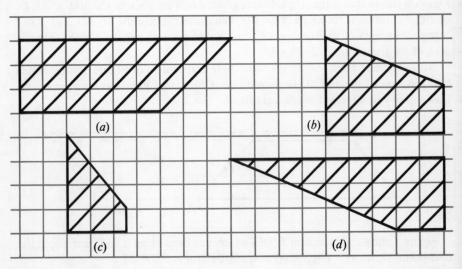

Fig. 9

2 Find the area of the following trapeziums in Figure 10.

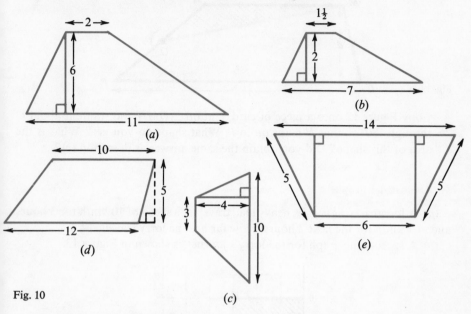

Fig. 10

3 In Figure 11 the diagrams represent the cross-sections of various buildings. Using any appropriate method calculate the areas of the cross-sections of these buildings.

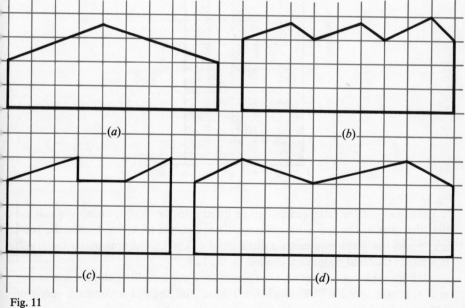

Fig. 11

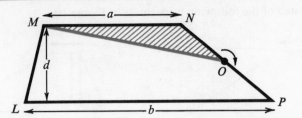

Fig. 12

4   Copy Figure 12 onto a piece of card. Cut off $\triangle OMN$ and rotate it about O through 180° so that N maps on to P. What shape do you get? What is the area of this shape? Did you obtain the same answer as in section (c)?

3   Areas under graphs

(a) A lorry carrying a wide, heavy load travels at a speed of 10 km/h for 3 hours and at 7 km/h for the next 2 hours. How far has the lorry travelled?

(b) A speed–time graph for the lorry's journey is shown in Figure 13.

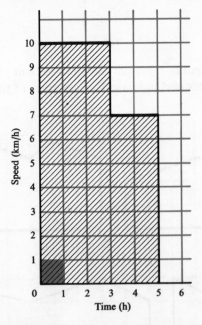

Fig. 13

How many of the red squares can be fitted into the shaded area? We can see that the area of the red square represents a distance of 1 km. Hence the total area under the graph represents a distance of 44 km, i.e. the area under the graph represents the total distance travelled by the lorry.

(c) Figure 14 shows a speed–time graph for a car travelling along a motorway at a constant speed of 100 km/h for 1 hour and then at a constant speed of 120 km/h for 2 hours.

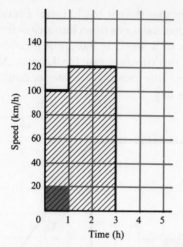

Fig. 14

Do you agree that the red square represents a distance of 20 km? How many of the red squares can be fitted into the shaded area? What is the total distance travelled by the car?

(*d*) The graphs in sections (*b*) and (*c*) represent idealized situations. Lorries and cars cannot, in fact, change speeds instantaneously as the graphs suggest. A more realistic description of the lorry's journey is represented by Figure 15.

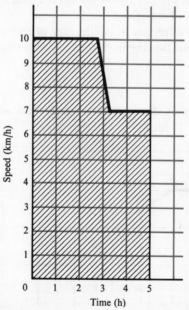

Fig. 15

Use the graph to describe the lorry's journey in words. Calculate the area under the graph and hence write down the distance the lorry travelled.

Now sketch a more realistic version of the car's journey than that represented by Figure 14. Do not forget that the car has to travel a total distance of 340 km.

(*e*) The rate at which industrial waste flows into a river from a factory increases during the first two hours of a working day until it reaches a maximum. The waste is then produced at this constant rate for 4 hours. After this it decreases. The graph in Figure 16 shows the amount of waste per hour flowing into the river at various times during the day.

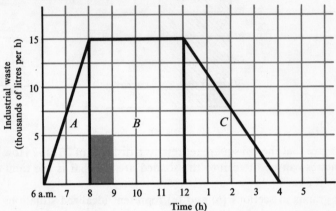

Fig. 16

The shaded rectangle represents a quantity of 5000 litres of industrial waste. The area of triangle A is $\frac{1}{2} \times 2 \times 15 = 15$. Thus the area of region A represents a quantity of 15 000 litres of waste.

Calculate (i) the area of region B; (ii) the area of region C. Hence write down the total amount of waste flowing from the factory per day.

Exercise C

1 A group of Vth formers start out on a charity walk across a National Park. The graph in Figure 17 illustrates their progress.

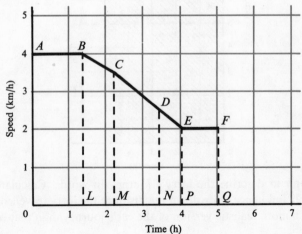

Fig. 17

Use the graph to answer the following questions:

(a) For how long did they walk at a speed of 4 km/h?

(b) What do the lines BC, CD, DE tell you?

(c) At what speed did they walk during the last hour?

(d) How far did they walk in the first 2 hours?

(e) If they were receiving a total of £2·65 per kilometre how much did they raise for charity?

2 Each diagram in Figure 18 shows part of a graph. What does the shaded area represent in each case?

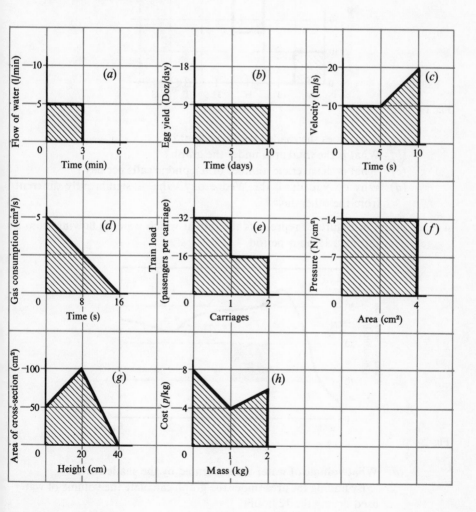

Fig. 18

3 Figure 19 shows the average number of telephone calls per day received by a shop in a normal working week.

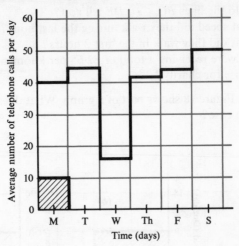

Fig. 19

(a) What does the shaded area represent?
(b) What is the total area under the graph?
(c) What is the average number of telephone calls per day?
(d) Why do you think the Wednesday value is significantly different from the other days?

4 The graph in Figure 20 represents the rate at which water is flowing from a reservoir during a 12 hour period.

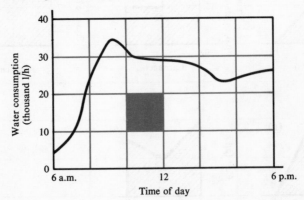

Fig. 20

(a) What volume of water is represented by the shaded area?
     By finding the area under the graph calculate the volume of water used during the 12 hours.
(b) Is more water used between 6 a.m. and 9 a.m. than between 3 p.m. and 6 p.m.?

(c) If water flows into the reservoir at a steady rate of 28 thousand litres per hour during the 12 hour period, will the water level be lower or higher at 6 p.m. than at 6 a.m.?

5 The graph in Figure 21 shows how a person's heart beat varied with time.

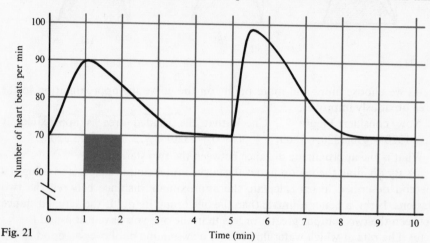

Fig. 21

Notice that the vertical scale starts at 60.

(a) What does the shaded square represent?
(b) Calculate the average heart beat for the first 'hump'.
(c) What was his normal heart beat? Calculate the average heart beat over the 10 minutes shown.

4 Areas under curves

(a)

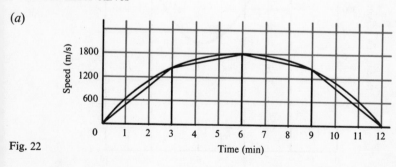

Fig. 22

Figure 22 is the speed–time graph of a train travelling from Reading to Twyford.

By dividing the region between the curve and the time axis into simple shapes we can approximate to the area under the curve. Figure 23 shows three ways of doing this.

179

Area of irregular shapes

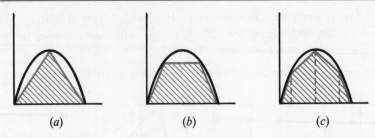

(a)   (b)   (c)

Fig. 23

As we choose more and more points on the curve the approximation to the area obviously improves.

Now consider Figure 22. Check that the shaded area is approximately
$\frac{1}{2}.3.1320 + \frac{1}{2}.3(1320 + 1800) + \frac{1}{2}.3(1800 + 1320) + \frac{1}{2}.3.1320 = 13\,320$.

What is the approximate distance between the two stations?

(b) By dividing the region under the curve into 6 simple shapes and using the method described in (a) calculate the approximate distance between the two stations. Is this a better estimate than the one found in (a)? Is the actual distance between the two stations greater or less than the one you have just found?

(c) The rate at which water flowed into a swimming pool over a period of ten minutes is shown in Figure 24.

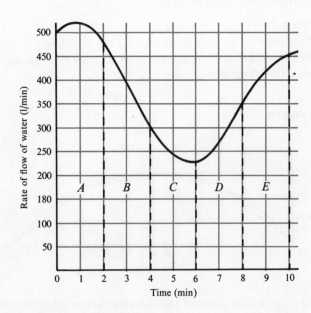

Fig. 24

The area under the curve is divided into five trapeziums of equal width and if we separate the trapeziums we obtain Figure 25.

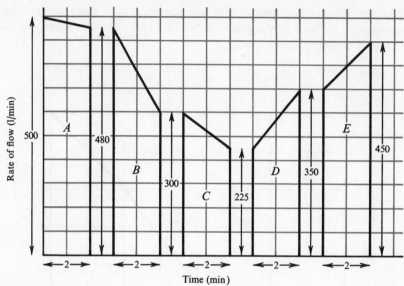

Fig. 25

Using the formula for the area of a trapezium we have:

Area $A = \frac{2}{2}(500 + 480) = 980$. A represents 980 litres.
Area $B = \frac{2}{2}(480 + 300) = 780$. B represents 780 litres.

Now find the area of the trapeziums C, D and E and hence find the number of litres that flowed into the swimming pool. Repeat the calculation by dividing the area into ten trapeziums of equal width.

Is this a better estimate of the number of litres in the pool?

Exercise D

1

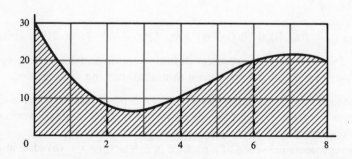

Fig. 26

Use the trapezium method to find the area under the graph shown above using (a) 2, (b) 4, (c) 8 trapeziums of equal width.

181

2 Find the velocity achieved in 200 seconds by a four stage rocket whose acceleration is given by the graph shown in Figure 27. (Note that, for each period of constant acceleration,

$$\text{acceleration} = \frac{\text{velocity}}{\text{time}}, \text{ so that acceleration} \times \text{time} = \text{velocity.})$$

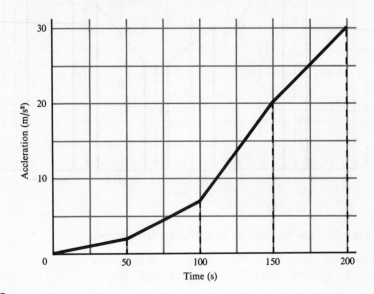

Fig. 27

3 The number of cars passing a factory over a 5 hour period was estimated from samples taken every half hour. (The number of cars passing in 6 minutes was counted and multiplied by 10 to find the hourly rate.) The results were as follows:

Time (a.m.) 7.00 7.30 8.00 8.30 9.00 9.30 10.00 10.30 11.00 11.30 noon
Number of
  cars per
  hour   700 1000 1800 3000 4000 4300 4200 3500 2100 1600 1400

Draw a smooth curve to represent this information and determine from it the total number of cars (to the nearest thousand) passing in the period.

4 Estimate the area enclosed between the graph (see Figure 28), the x axis and the lines $x = 4$, $x = 7$. Explain whether your method gives an over estimate or an under estimate of the true area.

If y represents the speed of a particle in m/s at time x s: (a) state in general terms what the particle is doing at the time interval shown; (b) state the physical significance of the area that you found in the first part of the question, expressing it in appropriate units.

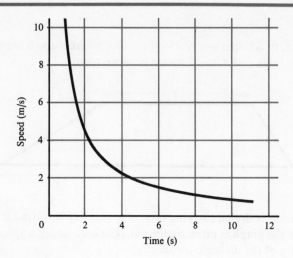

Fig. 28

5   The speed of an object is given by the formula $v = 2 + 3t$, where v is the speed in metres per second and t is the time in seconds. Complete a table of values for the speed for the first 10 seconds. Draw a graph of the function: time → speed. What is the gradient and what does it represent? By finding the appropriate areas under the graph calculate the distance travelled after 1, 2, 3, 4, 5, 6, 7, 8, 9, 10 seconds have elapsed. Use this information to draw a graph of time → distance travelled.

6   The table below shows the area of circles for a given radius.

Area A	3·14	12·55	28·2	50·03	78·5
Radius r	1	2	3	4	5

Copy and complete the following table:

Area		12·55		50·03	
$\dfrac{1}{r^2}$	1	0·85			

Draw a graph of the function: area → $\dfrac{1}{r^2}$. Join the points with a smooth curve and calculate the area beneath the curve. If the values of r were increased estimate the area under the curve.

Area of irregular shapes

Summary

1 The area, A, of a trapezium is $A = \frac{1}{2}(a + b)d$, where a and b are the lengths of the parallel sides and d, the distance between them.

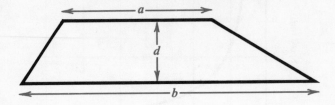

Fig. 29

2 When a graph is drawn showing how one quantity is related to another, the area under the graph is often significant. The area under a speed–time graph is a measure of the distance travelled.

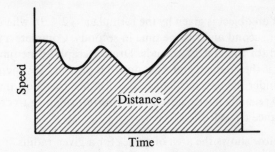

Fig. 30

3 When finding the area under a graph it is often helpful to divide the space into trapeziums: computation is much easier if the trapeziums are all of the same width.

184

Computing project

1 Communicating with a computer – input and output

(*a*) In order to make a computer work for us we must be able to communicate with it. You will already know that a computer operates under the control of a program. This program, along with the data to be processed must be *input* in a form that the computer can understand. When the data has been processed the computer must *output* information in a form intelligible to man, or in a form which can be used again as input material.

(b) Figure 1 shows a section of 5-track paper tape. Why do you think it is called '5-track tape'? You can see from the figure that each *column* of the tape

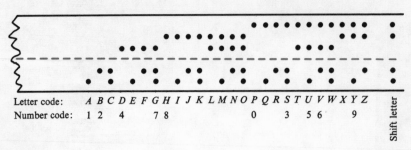

Fig. 1

represents one *character* (A, B, C, d, e, +, ;, ...). Information is punched column by column onto the tape and can be read by photoelectric cells, converted into machine language and input to the computer store.

(c) Use the code in Figure 1 to decipher the information on the cover of this book.

(d) Try to obtain some punched tape and punched cards (Figure 2) from a computer installation. Is it 8, 7, 6 or 5-track paper tape?

How many tracks have the cards in Figure 2? How many characters can each card hold?

Can you work out what is written on the card in Figure 2(b) by using the code on the card in Figure 2(a)?

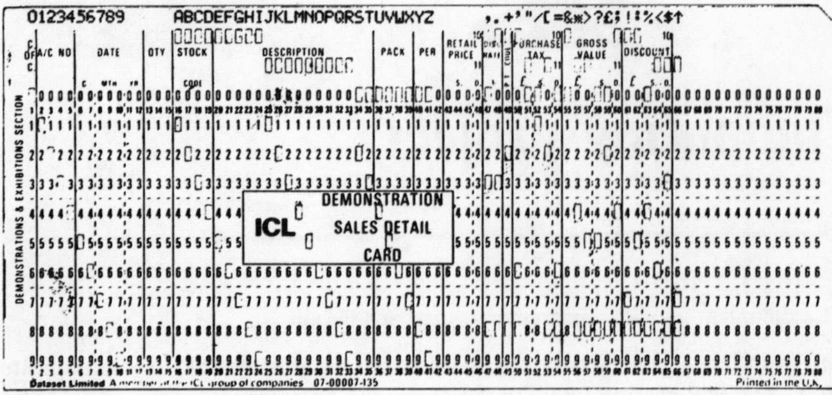

Fig. 2(a)

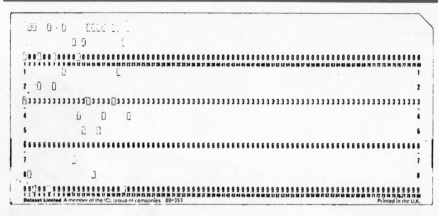

Fig. 2(b)

(e) Count the number of holes in each column of the paper tape in Figure 1. What do you notice? Find out what is meant by:

(i) parity;   (ii) a verifier;   (iii) letter shift.

How many different characters can be represented on (i) 8-track; (ii) 5-track paper tape?

(f) What do you think are the advantages and disadvantages of using punched cards as opposed to paper tape for input purposes?

(g) Punched cards and paper tape are examples of some of the earliest ways man devised for feeding a computer with information. Nowadays more sophisticated methods are being used alongside these two.

(h) Study the picture of the cheque in Figure 3. The cheque number is written in metallic ink. What do the other numbers represent? A machine called an 'optical scanner' is able to recognize characters written in this special way and so pass information to the computer. When cheques are cashed the computer is able to debit the correct amount by virtue of the code numbers. How does the

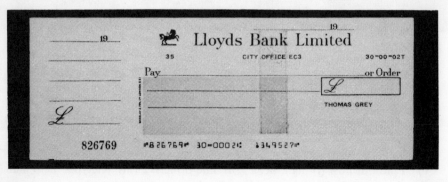

Fig. 3

computer know the *amount* to be debited? You will be able to obtain information from any local bank.

Fig. 4

(*i*) Figure 4 shows a visual display unit (VDU). VDU's are connected directly to the computer. Information from store can be relayed instantly onto the screen and displayed in written form.

The screen in the picture displays a person's electricity bill. By typing messages to the computer the operator can update the bill and return the updated information back into store.

(*j*) Find out how (i) 'light pens'; (ii) 'line printers'; (iii) 'teletypes' help man and computer to communicate with each other.

Control room – Houston, Texas

2 Computers at work

(*a*) Computers are used because of their high speed and reliability. Their task is to process information input to them, and to output results. The processing procedure can take many forms, from comparing criminals' crime patterns to working out monthly payrolls.

(*b*) The Chicago police use a computer to aid them in crime detection. Most criminals specialize in a particular type of crime and use a similar method every time they work. Information on known criminals is held in the computer store in the form of binary patterns. When a crime is committed the patterns for the crime are compared with those held in store. In this way suspects are selected and listed by the computer. The material is then used as a starting point in police enquiries.

(*c*) Many large firms now use a computer for 'stock control'. Each item in stock (say, for example, jars of jam) is allotted its own code number. A 'master file' (usually a magnetic tape, or disc) holds for each item: (i) the code number; (ii) the maximum quantity the warehouse should hold; (iii) the minimum quantity the warehouse should hold; (iv) the quantity held in stock at the end of the previous day's transactions.

The information from invoices is recorded on a transaction file, and processing takes the form of comparing code numbers, checking stock levels, and making adjustments to the master file where necessary. In this way a new master file is created each day. If the stock level for an item falls below the minimum level, the computer prints out a request for more stock. The diagram in Figure 5 will help to explain the procedure.

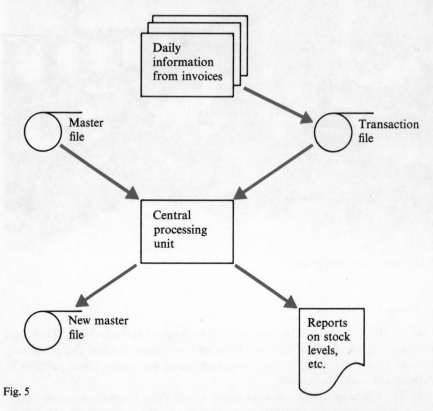

Fig. 5

(*d*) Computers are used by airlines to assist with booking arrangements. Details of flights and availability of seats are stored in a central computer. Booking offices throughout the country are linked to the computer by 'on line links' and requests for seats can be typed to the computer by teletype. The computer searches its records for available seats and advises as to availability or possible alternative arrangements via the 'on line link'. Once a booking has been made the records are automatically updated ready for the next call. In this way many people can gain access to the computer almost simultaneously and obtain information in a few seconds (only a minute fraction of this time is, in fact, taken up by the processing procedure).

(*e*) The above are just three ways in which computers are used in daily life. There are many more examples. Try to find out how computers are utilized in (i) hospitals; (ii) local government; (iii) factories, for machine control.

What is meant by (i) 'real time' processing; (ii) 'multiprogramming'?

Revision exercises

Slide rule session no. 5

Give all answers as accurately as your slide rule permits.

1 $3\cdot3 \times 24\cdot5$.	2 $19\cdot2 \times 7\cdot6$.	3 $(9\cdot4)^2$.
4 $17 \times 28\cdot9$.	5 $0\cdot59 \times 32$.	6 $24\cdot5 \div 3\cdot3$.
7 $7\cdot6 \div 19\cdot2$.	8 $9\cdot44 \div 1\cdot2$.	9 $28\cdot9 \div 17$.
10 $0\cdot59 \div 32$.		

Slide rule session no. 6

Give all answers as accurately as possible.

1 $\sqrt{51\cdot3}$.	2 $\sqrt{75\,000}$.	3 $(1\cdot91)^3$.
4 $\pi \times (2\cdot7)^2$.	5 $37 \times (0\cdot81)^2$.	6 $\frac{4}{3}\pi \times (1\cdot2)^3$.
7 $(23)^2 \times 19$.	8 $(0\cdot112)^3$.	9 $\dfrac{1\cdot21 \times 1\cdot06}{1\cdot12}$.
10 $24\cdot6 \times 19 \times 0\cdot07$.		

Slide rule session no. 7

1 $2\cdot16 \times 1\cdot62$.	2 $3\cdot03 \times 2\cdot53$.	3 $(2\cdot45)^2$.
4 π^2.	5 $0\cdot607 \times 0\cdot112$.	6 $2\cdot16 \div 1\cdot62$.
7 $3\cdot03 \div 2\cdot53$.	8 $2\cdot45 \div 8\cdot1$.	9 $\pi \div 3$.
10 $0\cdot607 \div 0\cdot112$.		

Trigonometry tables: practice

1   Use tables to find (*a*) $\sin 35°$, (*b*) $\sin 85\cdot5°$, (*c*) $\cos 47\cdot2°$.
2   Use tables to find x where

       (*a*) $\sin x° = 0\cdot421$,   (*b*) $\cos x° = 0\cdot037$,   (*c*) $\cos x° = 0\cdot980$.

3   Calculate $2 \sin 17° + \cos 17°$.
4   Find θ if $\sin \theta° = \frac{3}{4}$.
5   Calculate $1/\sin 20\cdot8°$.
6   Calculate, and then add, the squares of (*a*) $\sin 64°$, (*b*) $\cos 64°$.
7   Find the coordinates of P, given that $OP = 5$ and OP makes an angle of $40°$ with $y = 0$.
8   In the triangle ABC, $\angle BAC = 90°$, $ACB = 21°$, $BC = 5$ cm. Find AB and AC.

Revision exercises

Exercise E

1 Give the interquartile range of the numbers 4, 6, 7, 9, 10, 15, 19.

2 Thirteen people asked to guess the mass of a cake to the nearest half-kilo gave the following answers: $3\frac{1}{2}$, $2\frac{1}{2}$, 2, 1, $3\frac{1}{2}$, 2, $3\frac{1}{2}$, 3, 3, 1, $1\frac{1}{2}$, $2\frac{1}{2}$, $3\frac{1}{2}$ kg. What is (a) the modal value, (b) the median value, (c) the mean value?

3 Calculate x and y if $\begin{pmatrix} x \\ y \end{pmatrix} = \begin{pmatrix} 2 & 1 \\ 3 & -1 \end{pmatrix}\begin{pmatrix} 1 \\ 3 \end{pmatrix}$.

4 State the probability that a throw of a die will result in a score of 3 or more.

5 $\mathbf{a} = \begin{pmatrix} 1 \\ 2 \\ 3 \\ 4 \end{pmatrix}$; $\mathbf{b} = \begin{pmatrix} 2 \\ 4 \\ 6 \\ 8 \end{pmatrix}$; $\mathbf{c} = \begin{pmatrix} 1 \\ 3 \\ 5 \\ 7 \end{pmatrix}$.

Find (a) $5\mathbf{a}$; (b) $\frac{1}{2}\mathbf{b}$; (c) $3\mathbf{c}$; (d) $\mathbf{a} + \mathbf{c}$; (e) $\mathbf{b} + \mathbf{c}$; (f) $\mathbf{c} + \mathbf{b}$; (g) $3\mathbf{a} + 3\mathbf{b}$; (h) $3(\mathbf{b} + \mathbf{a})$.

6 Write down a set of five integers:

    (a) whose mean is 7 and whose median is 5;
    (b) whose median is 7 and whose mean is 5.

7 State a fraction whose value lies between $\frac{1}{2}$ and $\frac{4}{9}$.

8 State the number 0·073 46 correct to three significant figures.

In Questions 9 and 10 say which statements are true and which are false.

9 If $p = 12_5, q = 24_5$ and $r = 24_5$, then:

    (a) $q < r$;   (b) $q = 2p$;   (c) $p + q = 42$;   (d) $5q = 240_5$.

10 If $\mathbf{P}$ denotes reflection in $y = 0$, and $\mathbf{Q}$ denotes reflection in $x = 4$, and if Z is the point $(^-1, 3)$, then:

    (a) $\mathbf{P}(Z) = (^-1, ^-3)$;   (b) $\mathbf{Q}(Z) = (^-1, 1)$;
    (c) $\mathbf{PQ}(Z) = (^-9, 3)$;   (d) $\mathbf{PQ} = \mathbf{QP}$;
    (e) $\mathbf{P}^2 = \mathbf{I}$ (where $\mathbf{I}$ is the identity transformation).

Exercise F

1 Find the value of $\dfrac{ab}{c}$, where $a = 10^6, b = 10^7, c = 10^{-3}$.

2 If $a * b$ denotes $a + 2b$, calculate $3 * 2$ and $2 * 3$.

3 What do the results of Question 2 show about the nature of the operation $*$?

4   A book is being checked for printing errors; the reader finds that the number of mistakes per page is as follows:

No. of mistakes	0	1	2	3	4	5	6	7	Total
No. of pages	24	36	18	12	4	3	2	1	100

What is the modal value? Draw a cumulative frequency graph and mark on it the median value. Calculate the mean value. How do the three averages compare?

5   Write down an ordered set of five integers whose mean is 4 and whose median is 3.

6   What is the effect of the matrix $\begin{pmatrix} 2 & 1 \\ 1 & 2 \end{pmatrix}$ upon the square whose vertices are $(0,0)$; $(1,0)$; $(1,1)$; $(0,1)$?

7   Mark the points: $A(2,2)$; $B(3,4)$; $C(5,5)$; $D(6,2)$; $E(4,1)$.

(a)   Write down the vectors of the translations such that

(i) $A \to B$; (ii) $B \to C$; (iii) $C \to D$; (iv) $D \to E$; (v) $E \to A$.

(b)   Add these 5 vectors. Is the result what you expected?

8   Solve the following equations:

(a) $\dfrac{30}{x} - 11 = 19$;   (b) $2\left(3 + \dfrac{4}{x}\right) = 22$.

9   A boy very much wanted a mongrel puppy. His parents said he could have it if it could be trained within a school holiday (30 days). To persuade them, the boy asked mongrel owners he knew how long they had taken to train their dogs. These answers in days were:

20   31   45   18   28   17   23   30   35   42   21   37
24   26   34   18   27   16   12   33   23   27   26

He decided to find the mean and the median and to show the answer more favourable to his argument. He then decided to show some measure of scatter or deviation. He worked out the inter-quartile range.
   Draw a cumulative frequency diagram and mark on it the mean, median and quartiles.
   Briefly state the boy's argument to be allowed to keep the puppy.

10   Graph the function $x \to x^2$ for $x = {}^-3, {}^-2\frac{1}{2}, {}^-2, \ldots, 2, 2\frac{1}{2}, 3$. Join the points with a smooth curve and hence estimate the value of $\sqrt{5}$.

Revision exercises

Exercise G

1 Solve $2m - 7 = 3$.
2 Solve $9(k + 3) = 18$.
3 Simplify $\varnothing \cap \mathscr{E}$.
4 Simplify $A \cup A'$.
5 If $f(x) = 2 + x$, find $f^{-1}(0)$.
6 If $f(x) = x^2 + 3x + 1$, find $f(4)$.
7 The following table shows the heights, to the nearest cm, of a sample of 124 seedling fir trees:

Height	11	12	13	14	15	16	17	18	19	20	21
Number	5	9	14	18	20	17	18	13	6	3	1

Find the mean, median and quartiles.

8 Two dice are made in the shape of regular tetrahedra and have the numbers 1, 2, 3, 4 inscribed on their four faces. Make a table to show all the possible combinations of the scores on the hidden two faces when the dice are thrown together. What are the probabilities of the total scores being: (a) 2, (b) 5, (c) 9?

9 Show that the matrices $\mathbf{M}$ and $\mathbf{I}$ where $\mathbf{M} = \begin{pmatrix} -1 & 2 \\ 0 & 3 \end{pmatrix}$ and $\mathbf{I} = \begin{pmatrix} 1 & 0 \\ 0 & 1 \end{pmatrix}$ satisfy the equation $\mathbf{M}^2 - 2\mathbf{M} - 3\mathbf{I} = 0$.

10 If the matrices $\mathbf{X} = \begin{pmatrix} 1 & 1 \\ 0 & 1 \end{pmatrix}$ and $\mathbf{Y} = \begin{pmatrix} 1 & 0 \\ 1 & 1 \end{pmatrix}$ represent transformations, find the matrices $\mathbf{X}^2$, $\mathbf{Y}^2$, $\mathbf{XY}$ and $\mathbf{YX}$. Use a graph to show the effect of these combined transformations on the unit square.

Exercise H

1 $(2, 1)$, $(2, {}^-1)$, $({}^-2, {}^-1)$, $({}^-2, 1)$ are the vertices of a quadrilateral. Find its area.
2 Find the distances of the other vertices of the quadrilateral in Question 1 from the vertex $(2, 1)$.
3 Describe the shape of the region $\{(x, y): 3 < x < 5\} \cap \{(x, y): 0 < y < 2\}$.
4 If a square and a circle have the same perimeter, which has the greater area?
5 $ABCD$ is a square, with the diagonals AC and BD drawn in. Is the figure traversable?
6 A football moves from A to E by passes described by the following vectors:

$$\mathbf{AB} = \begin{pmatrix} 4 \\ 3 \end{pmatrix}, \quad \mathbf{BC} = \begin{pmatrix} -3 \\ 4 \end{pmatrix}, \quad \mathbf{CD} = \begin{pmatrix} 2 \\ 0 \end{pmatrix}, \quad \mathbf{DE} = \begin{pmatrix} 5 \\ -1 \end{pmatrix}.$$

Calculate the vector $\mathbf{AE}$, and indicate the ball's motion on a diagram. Calculate the length of AE.

7   If $g: x \rightarrow 1 + \dfrac{x}{2}$, express the function g^{-1} in the same form and find the value of $g^{-1}g^{-1}(2)$. Check your answer by finding the function gg and using the fact that $(gg)^{-1} = g^{-1}g^{-1}$. For what value of x does $gg(x) = 101$?

8   Represent on number lines, the intersection of the solution sets for each of the following pairs:

   (a) $3 - x < 5$ and $5 < 4 - x$;   (b) $\dfrac{x+1}{2} \leqslant 1$ and $1 \leqslant x + 3$.

9   Is the shaded area in Figure 1:

   (a) $(X \cup Y) \cap Z$;   (b) $(X \cap Y) \cup Z$;
   (c) $(X \cap Y') \cap Z$;   (d) $(X \cap Y)' \cap Z$?

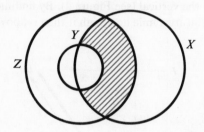

Fig. 1

10   If $\mathscr{E} = \{10, 11, 12, 13, 14, 15, 16, 17, 18, 19\}$, list the members of the following subsets of $\mathscr{E}$:

   (a) {prime numbers};
   (b) {multiples of 3};
   (c) {numbers such that $55 - 2x = 25$};
   (d) {numbers such that $(x - 13)^2 = 4$}.

List the members of any two subsets A and B of $\mathscr{E}$ such that $A \cap B = \varnothing$, and $A \cup B = \mathscr{E}$.

Exercise I

1   Simplify $\frac{7}{8} \div \frac{3}{4}$.
2   Express 1111_2 in base 8.
3   One side of a right-angled triangle is 4 cm long and the hypotenuse is 5 cm long. Find the area of the triangle.
4   (a) Does $x = 3$ satisfy the relation $3x - 5 < \frac{1}{2}(2x + 1)$?
   (b) What can you say about x if $2x + 5 > 5x + 17$?
   (c) Solve $4(3 - x) < 30$.
5   In a village of 176 houses it is discovered that the only newspapers that anyone buys are the *Daily Telegraph*, *Daily Mail* and the *Mirror*. The newsagent delivers at least one paper to every house, but never 2 copies of

the same paper to one house. Altogether they deliver 40 copies of the *Mirror*, 71 *Telegraphs* and 98 *Mails*. Including those houses that take all three papers, 12 take the *Mirror* and the *Mail*, 13 take the *Mail* and the *Telegraph*, and 15 take the *Telegraph* and *Mirror*. Draw a Venn diagram and hence find how many take all three.

6   (*a*) Write down all the subsets with three elements of the set b_1, b_2, b_3, b_4 and the subsets with two elements of the set g_1, g_2, g_3. (*b*) If three boys are chosen at random from Bryan, Basil, Benjamin and Bartholomew and two girls from Gloria, Grace and Gladys, what is the probability that neither Bryan nor Grace are chosen? What is the probability that Bryan, Basil, Gloria and Grace are chosen?

7   A rocket rises 15 km vertically, 20 km at 30° from the vertical, and then 50 km at 35° from the vertical (see Figure 2). By finding the lengths *BE* and *EF* calculate to the nearest mile how high it then is above the launching pad.

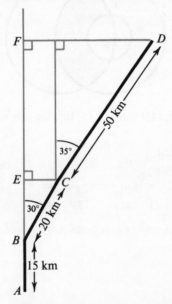

Fig. 2

8   Here are the brands of toothpaste used by the boys of one form: 12 use Bitewite, 9 use Shynodent, 6 use Tusko, 4 use Formula XT 5, 3 use Molarcare, 2 use Toothine. Illustrate this information by: (*a*) a bar chart, (*b*) a pie chart.

9   Mark the points $A(4, 5)$, $B(2, 1)$ and $C(4, 0)$ on graph paper.

(*a*)   Show on your diagram the result of applying the translation $\begin{pmatrix} -2 \\ 1 \end{pmatrix}$ to *ABC*. Label this *A'B'C'*.

(*b*)   *A'B'C'* is now rotated through 60° anticlockwise about *O*. Construct the image of *A'B'C'* and label it *A"B"C"*.

(c) Find by construction the centre of the rotation that maps ABC straight onto $A''B''C''$.

10 A helicopter flies due north at 180 kilometres per hour for 1 hour. It then changes course to due east and continues for 20 minutes. On what course should it fly to return directly to the starting point and how long will this take if the same speed is maintained?

Exercise J

1 Find the solution set of each of the following:

(a) $2(3x - 1) + 8 = 6(x + 1)$;   (b) $1 - (4 - x) > x - 2$.

2 10022 is a number in the base of three, and the same number is represented as 155 in another base. What is the base?

3 Let A be the point $(3,0)$, B the point $(6,5)$ and C the point $(3,5)$. If the line through C parallel to BA meets the line $y = 0$ at D, what are the coordinates of D?

4 Draw a figure, like an F, in an equilateral triangle. Draw its images under reflection in the three sides of the triangle. What transformations connect these images?

5 Figure 3 shows three networks. List the number of nodes (N), arcs (A) and regions (R), and so verify Euler's relation $R + N = A + 2$ for each network. Does this relation hold for Figure 3 considered as a whole?

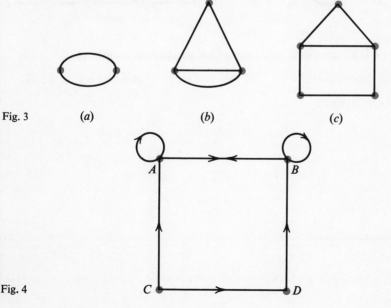

Fig. 3   (a)   (b)   (c)

Fig. 4   C   D

6 (a) Compile a direct-route matrix **S** for the network shown in Figure 4. Why is it not symmetrical about the leading diagonal? (b) Find the matrix **S²**. What does it represent?

7 Say whether each statement is true or false; and where one is false suggest how it could be amended.

    (a) π is exactly $\frac{22}{7}$;

    (b) $0.9^2 < 0.9$;

    (c) in base 5, 302 is an even number;

    (d) a cube has three planes of symmetry.

8 Find the area of the Meccano piece shown in Figure 5, given that the radii of the large arcs are 2·7 and 3·8 cm, that the ends are semi-circles and the holes have diameters of 0·25 cm. (Take π to be 3·14.)

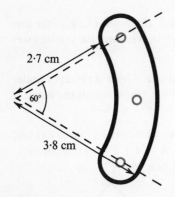

2·7 cm

60°

3·8 cm

Fig. 5

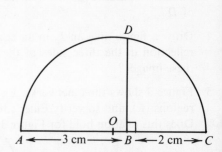

D

$A \longleftarrow 3\ cm \longrightarrow B \longleftarrow 2\ cm \longrightarrow C$

O

Fig. 6

9 Figure 6 is a semi-circle with centre O. Calculate the lengths of

    (a) the radius OD;   (b) the arc DC;   and find (c) $\angle BOD$.

(Take $\pi = 3\cdot14$).

Index

Index